THE MICHIGAN SOLDIERS & SAILORS MONUMENT.

DETROIT, 1872.

THE CALVERT LITH. CO. DETROIT.

THE

FLAGS OF MICHIGAN.

COMPILED BY

JNO. ROBERTSON,

Adjutant General.

LANSING, MICH.:
W. S. GEORGE & CO., STATE PRINTERS AND BINDERS.
1877.

STATE MILITARY OFFICERS.

Governor CHARLES M. CROSWELL, Commander-in-Chief.

Brigadier General JOHN ROBERTSON, Adjutant General March 15, 1861.

Brigadier General LEMUEL SAVIERS, Quartermaster General, May 21st, 1877.

Brigadier General LEWIS W. HEATH, Inspector General, March 8th, 1877.

Major GEORGE C. SMITH, Military Secretary, July 1st, 1877.

Major WILLIAM C. FITZSIMMONS, Judge Advocate, October 1st, 1877.

AIDS TO COMMANDER-IN-CHIEF.

Colonel GROVER S. WORMER, October 1st, 1877; Colonel JAMES O'DONNELL, October 1st, 1877; Colonel EDWIN S. PIERCE, October 1st, 1877; Colonel WILLIAM JENNY, JR., October 1st, 1877.

STATE MILITARY BOARD.

CHARLES E. GRISSON, September 23d, 1873; HENRY M. DUFFIELD, February 28th, 1874; LEWIS W. HEATH, March 8th, 1877.

"Stand by the flag, on land, and ocean billow,
By it your fathers stood, unmoved and true,
Living, defended, dying, from their pillow,
With their last blessing, passed it on to you."

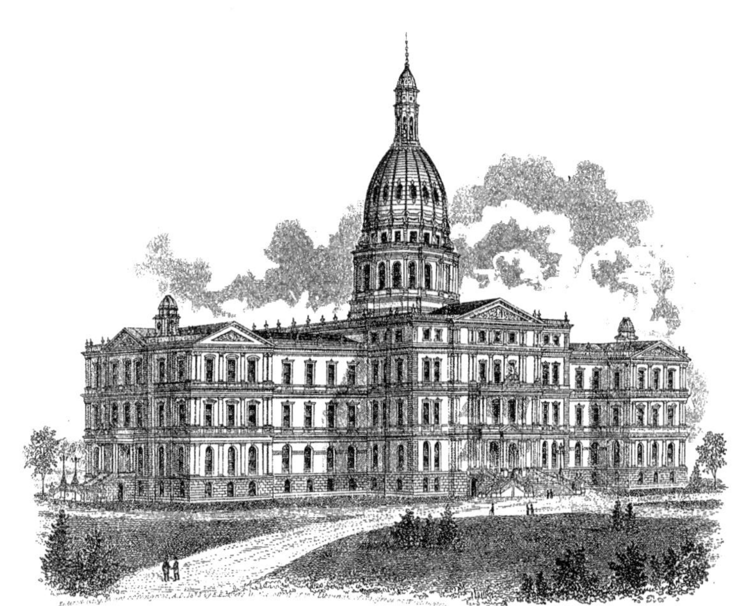

E. E. MYERS, ARCHITECT. THE CALVERT LITH. CO. DETROIT.

STATE CAPITOL
LANSING.

FLAGS OF MICHIGAN.

MILITARY DEPARTMENT, MICHIGAN,
ADJUTANT GENERAL'S OFFICE,
Detroit, February 12, 1877.

GOVERNOR:—Anticipating the early deposit of the "War Flags" of Michigan in the capitol at Lansing, and recognizing the necessity for placing their record with them, I beg respectfully to submit the accompanying brief history on the subject, trusting that you will give it such direction as will bring about its publication, in such manner as may be deemed best.

Very respectfully,
Your most obedient servant,
JNO. ROBERTSON,
Adjutant General.

Governor CHARLES M. CROSWELL,
Lansing, Mich.

EXECUTIVE OFFICE,
Lansing, May 17, 1877.

To the Legislature:

I herewith submit a communication from the Adjutant General of the State, accompanied by a brief but valuable sketch or record of the "War Flags of Michigan." It is anticipated that these Flags will be deposited in the new capitol on its completion, and it seems fitting and proper that every important circumstance connected with their history should be recorded and preserved.

Many of them are mere shreds, tattered, torn, and bullet-pierced, which illustrate the valor of the men of Michigan, as well as the important part the State has borne in some of the great wars of the United States, especially in the war with Mexico, and in the more recent struggle for the maintenance and preservation of the National Union.

Beneath their folds more than ninety thousand of the bravest sons of the State pressed forward through privations and amid dangers, to share largely and gloriously in nearly all the battles of the great rebellion. With unyielding devotion many gave up their lives that the nation might live, while the bleeding wounds and the trials and sufferings of others attested their fidelity to the Union and their valor in its behalf. And when their work was accomplished, in the day of their triumph, treasuring no spirit of resentment, with moderation unsurpassed, these heroes freely forgave their enemies, and restoring peace on unparalleled terms of generosity to the vanquished, betook themselves again to the quiet pursuits of life, by energy, industry, and thrift, to renew prosperity, and make good the waste of war.

These Battle-Flags are mementoes of patriotism and heroism worthy of remembrance, and their history should be carefully and gratefully cherished and preserved. I therefore respectfully recommend that the Legislature take such action, by concurrent resolution, as shall provide for the publication of the history, as a legislative document, in proper and suitable form.

CHARLES M. CROSWELL.

In response to this message, the committees on military and on printing of the Senate, through their chairmen, Messrs. L. J. Taylor and F. H. Rankin, reported the following preamble and concurrent resolution, which were unanimously adopted, by both houses of the Legislature:

Whereas, His Excellency the Governor has transmitted to the Legislature a communication from the Adjutant General of the State, accompanied by a record of the War Flags of Michigan, and recommends that the Legislature take such action by concurrent resolution as shall provide for the publication of the history of these mementoes of the patriotism and heroism of our citizen soldiers in proper and suitable form for preservation and distribution; therefore,

Resolved by the Senate (the House of Representatives concurring), That there be and the same is hereby ordered printed in a style similar to the printed proceedings of the Laying of the Corner Stone of the Michigan State Capitol, two thousand copies of the History of the Battle Flags of Michigan, at a cost not to exceed four hundred and fifty dollars,—one thousand copies for the use of State officers, members of the Legislature and officers of the same, and of the several State Boards, and one thousand copies for general distribution, as the Governor may direct.

From the earliest periods, flags and banners have been adopted and employed to designate nations, commonwealths, associations, clans, and families, as well as orders of nobility, one from another, by various colors, forms, symbols, and mottoes, and their composite has been as diversified as their use has been universal.

As emblems, they are revered and loved by the people in all countries, and exert a powerful influence in upholding unity and strength in nations and States, as well as in lesser compacts and associations.

In politics, they designate the various parties, and have much significance in processions, and other public gatherings, at the same time constituting a very interesting part of the display.

They form a portion of the equipment of all armies and navies, and although in peace they are usually erroneously regarded as merely for display, yet in war, they assume an importance and value which can only be fully appreciated by those who follow and fight under them. They often prove a more powerful incentive than the truest valor, and in the smoke and din of battle, when commands are silenced, and tactics and strategy fail, are the guiding stars, often leading armies on to glorious victory.

In our own country, the love and reverence for the old Flag were powerful incitements to patriotic action in the recent war, often leading those in the field to follow it to deeds of heroism not surpassed in any other war, while it aided much in strengthening and uniting the people in the determination to maintain the unity of the republic.

It is claimed as being well settled, that so far as recorded, the earliest Flags planted on North American shores, were those of England, and that with changing devices, various symbols and mottoes, they were continued through the provincial and colonial times, in the Anglo Saxon settlements, until the raising of the great union banner at Cambridge, Massachusetts, on January 2d, 1776. This contained the thirteen stripes of alternate red and white, as an emblem of the union of the thirteen colonies against the oppressive acts of Great Britain, but still retaining the blended crosses of Saint George and Saint Andrew. Soon after this, however, they were erased and a canopy of stars on a blue field substituted, thereby adding beauty and meaning to the fact that the last semblance of loyalty to England was to be renounced, an entire separation of the colonies from Great Britain effected, and the advent of a new power, which had by declaration a short time previous, proclaimed a free and independent state, to be known as the United States of America.

Symbolic ensigns, standards, and banners enter into the heraldry of all nations, but differ much in design; some have birds and fishes, some beasts, and others trees, while many have various other devices, and each with some adopted significance.

The "Stars and Stripes" were chosen for America. Opinions vary as to their meaning. Some say that the red is emblematic of the blood shed for our country by the forefathers, that the blue tells of the heavens, and their protection, while the stars represent the several States as one nationality.

The designating stripes on the coats of the Continental soldiers are said to have furnished the idea of the stripes, and some have supposed that they were borrowed from the Dutch, while others have believed that both stars and stripes were suggested by the Arms of Washington, which singularly contain both.

The designer of this union of stars is unfortunately unknown, but the eloquent and chaste significance applied to them is sublime. A new constellation, speaking of union, perpetuity, justice, equality, subordination, courage, and purity, with a covenant against oppression and in favor of liberty.

"For the hand that has woven those colors of light,
And sent it aflame thro' the World's every zone,
That has led, and has kept it thro' storm and thro' night,
Is the hand that has blest us, sweet Liberty's own!"

The star in the American banner, having only five points, seems to have been taken from either the heraldry of France, Germany, or Holland, while that on our coin, follows that of England, having six points.

On the 14th of June, 1777, the American Congress "*Resolved,* That the flag of the thirteen United States be thirteen stripes, alternate red and white; that the union be thirteen stars, white in a blue field, representing a new constellation."

This is the first and only legislative action, of which there is any record, for the establishment of a national Flag for the sovereign United States of America, declared independent July 4th, 1776, and proclaims the official birth of a new constellation as the symbol of their union. This dilatory resolve of congress, it will be observed, was not passed until eighteen months after the union Flag raising at Cambridge, and the sailing of the first American fleet from Philadelphia, under colonial colors, nearly a year after the declaration of the entire separation of the colonies from Great Britain.

After a number of additional States had been admitted to the union, a resolution was offered in Congress appointing a committee to inquire into the expediency of altering the flag of the United States. This committee reported a bill on the 2d of January, 1817, but it was not acted upon. On the re-assembling of Congress on the 16th of December following, the resolution was renewed, and on the 6th of January, 1818, a committee reported the following law, which was enacted and approved April 4th, 1818:

"AN ACT to establish the Flag of the United States.

"SECTION 1. Be it enacted, etc., that from and after the fourth day of July next, the flag of the United States be thirteen horizontal stripes, alternate red and white; that the union have twenty stars, white on a blue field.

"SEC. 2. And be it further enacted, that on the admission of every new State into the union, one star be added to the union of the Flag; and that such addition shall take effect on the fourth of July next succeeding such admission."

The Flag, it is claimed, was designated by Captain S. C. Reid, for which he received a vote of thanks from Congress in 1859. He had been the commander of a privateer, known as the "General Armstrong," and had defended her with much gallantry while being attacked by a British squadron of boats in Fayal Roads. He died in 1861, a Master in the United States Navy.

The first Flag is said to have been made at New York, by Mrs. S. C. Reid, under the direction of her husband, and to have been hoisted on the House of Representatives on the 13th of April, 1818, although the act establishing it was not to take effect until the fourth of July following.

It is also claimed that Mrs. John Ross was the first maker, and partial designer of the Stars and Stripes; that the house where the Flag was made is still standing, being 239 Arch St., Philadelphia; that she was visited by General Washington and a committee of Congress in June, 1776, who engaged her to make the Flag, from a rough drawing, and which, according to her suggestions, was re-drawn by General Washington in pencil, changing the formation of the stars from six cornered to five cornered.

It is said that a standard was presented to the Philadelphia troop of Light horse, by Captain Abraham Markoe, in 1774–5, and is still displayed at their anniversary dinners, and which is generally believed to be the first instance of the thirteen stripes being used upon an American Flag.

Capt. Nicholas Johnson, of Newburyport, master of the ship "*Count de Grasse*," is reported to have first displayed the stars and stripes as the American ensign on the river Thames, Connecticut; but the honor has since been claimed in behalf of a barque named the Maria, afterwards engaged in the whaling trade, and which was still in use in 1856, having returned to New Bedford, Massachusetts, in that year, undoubtedly the oldest vessel in America.

Paul Jones is accredited with being the man to first raise them as the Flag of America on a naval vessel named The Alfred, and in 1777 to have received the first salute for it in European waters, although opinions are advanced that the ship Bedford, of Nantucket, Capt. Wm. Mooers, should have the honor of first displaying the Flag in a British port.

After the signing of the Declaration of Independence, on the 4th of July, 1776, the Continental Congress, before adjourning on that day, appointed Dr. Franklin, Mr. Adams, and Mr. Jefferson as a committee to prepare a device for a seal of the United States. On August the 20th, following, they made a report, which was laid on the table.

In the Congress of the Confederation, on the 20th of June, 1782, the following "device for an armorial achievement, and reverse of the great seal for the United States in Congress assembled," was adopted.

Arms: "Paleways of thirteen pieces, argent and gules; a chief, azure; the escutcheon on the breast of the American eagle displayed proper, holding in his dexter talon an olive branch, and in his sinister a bundle of thirteen arrows, all proper, and in his beak a scroll inscribed with this motto: '*E pluribus unum.*'"

For the Crest: "Over the head of the eagle, which appears above the escutcheon, a glory, or breaking through a cloud, proper, and surrounding thirteen stars, forming a constellation, argent, on an azure field."

Reverse: "A pyramid unfinished. In the zenith, an eye in a triangle surrounded with glory, proper. Over the eye these words; '*Annuit cœptis.*' On the base of the pyramid the numerical letters, 'MDCCLXXVI;' and underneath the following motto: '*Novus ordo seclorum.*' "

In September, 1789, an act was passed and approved, which included, "That the seal heretofore used by the United States in Congress assembled, shall be, and hereby is, declared to be the seal of the United States."

The Arms are inscribed on what is used by the United States troops as the regimental or battalion color, made either of blue, yellow, or scarlet silk, designating the different arms of service, and are carried with the National Flag, constituting the colors of a regiment.

The principal figure on the Arms is the "national emblem,"—the bald or white headed eagle, one of the largest of his species, as he is the most beautiful of his tribe, while he is said to renew his age, and to exceed man in his length of days.*

As a bearing in a coat of armor, he is reckoned as honorable among birds, as the lion is among beasts. Although Dr. Franklin is said to have protested against adopting him as the emblem of America, saying; "For my part I wish the bald eagle had not been chosen as the representative of our country. He is a bird of bad moral character; he does not get his living honestly."

Notwithstanding this objection by Franklin, the eagle has always constituted a prominent feature in the heraldry of nations, and was at an early day made the imperial standard of the Romans, and from his aspiring flight and majestic soaring was fabled to hold communion with heaven, and to be the favorite messenger of Jove.

The Tartars have a particular esteem for the feathers of his tail, with which they superstitiously think to plume invincible arrows.

He is the venerated "great war eagle" of the northern and

* One of them is said to have died at Vienna after being in confinement for one hundred and four years.

western aborigines, and his caudal feathers are extremely valued for talismanic head dresses, and as sacred decorations for the "pipe of peace."

In the mode of getting his living, which nature gave him, and for which he cannot be held responsible, his moral character does not suffer much, in a comparison with that of the lion, the cherished emblem of a people, whose taste in such a choice, their American descendants, to some extent, may be excusable in following.

A beautiful idea is conveyed with regard to the American Flag, in the remarks of a little boy, whose parents resided near Bardstown, Kentucky, when a Michigan regiment was stationed there. Although very young, a mere child really, he had learned the difference in the appearance of union and confederate soldiers, having seen both, and he had also taken notice of the colors that composed the Flags of both. One morning discovering a beautiful rainbow arching the heavens, suspended as it were from the sky, he hurried to his mother, exclaiming with great earnestness, pointing upwards with both his little hands, "Mother! mother! Oh mother! God is a union man." His mother questioned him as to his reasons for thinking so, he replied, while a glow of delight flashed on his countenance, his little eyes beaming with brightness, "I know he is a union man, mother, for I have seen his Flag in heaven, and it is red, white, and blue."

During the life of the Republic, and especially during the late war, the National Flag has been gallantly defended, protected, and maintained, but perhaps never under such circumstances, or against such fearful odds, as was the Flag of Sumter, and certainly never, while initiating an era, involving such momentous results.

"We spiked the guns we left behind, and cut the flagstaff down—
From its top should float no color, if it might not hold our own."

From Fort Moultrie, in the darkness of the night, a little

band of heroes betake themselves to boats, bid farewell to their union home, and seek another in Charleston bay, reaching Sumter long ere the dawn had come, and at noon, on their knees in prayer, they again fling to the breeze the stars and stripes of Moultrie. Many days this little band witnessed the frowning batteries arise all around them. At length the rebel work of preparation is complete; they are summoned to surrender. Anderson replies, "Neither my sense of honor, nor my obligation to the government, will permit me to comply." The Flag that had been lowered with the coming on of night, is raised in the heavens. The posterns are closed. The men sit down in darkness to await the coming shock. With the early dawn comes the expected shot, and, like the deep thunder, awakes the morning echoes, and rolls over the trembling waters of the bay. No single shot before ever bore such destinies on its darkened flight.

They defend it for many days. The Fortress is fired with hot shot and exploding shell; the walls crumbling; the last biscuit gone; the main gate burned down; the conflict hopeless; still Anderson stands unmoved amid the wreck. The magazine on fire; the shell explode; the flagstaff is shot away; but in a rain of shot and shell, it is nailed to the ramparts, and the Flag waves defiantly until saluted by union guns, when the brave men march out to the music of the union, under the glorious "Old Flag,"—lowered, but not surrendered. Soon they are afloat on their ocean home, and the Flag of Sumter flutters proudly from the mast of the Baltic.

That unparalleled defense established the highest standard of patriotism and bravery, nerving every soldier to emulate the example. It planted in the true American heart, strong faith in the final success of the union cause, while the replacement of the identical Flag on the ruins, after four years of a gigantic and vigorous war, ending in complete victory, was a glorious triumph for the "Old Flag."

At Gettysburg, the great battle of the rebellion, Michigan troops were in large proportion. There the Confederate army of Virginia, and the Federal army of the Potomac, meet face to face; there the blue, under the star-spangled banner, and the grey, under the stars and bars, cover the hillocks and hillsides in that quiet green valley of the Keystone State.

> "Thin curling in the morning air
> The wreaths of failing smoke declare,
> To embers now the brands decayed
> Where the night watch their fires had made."

Out of the woodlands at break of day, a bullet comes ever and anon, an ominous messenger of the coming storm; no enemy is yet in sight; at last a grey line of men shoots up, then comes a shock of musketry that rakes the Seminary, rends the trees, and makes gaps in lines of carbineers. Men on stretchers pass in solemn round, and the great battle is surely and furiously on. On they come,

> "True to the last of their blood and their breath,
> And like reapers advance to the harvest of death."

Desperation is in their movements, they seem to hazard all, columns in mass rush on the union line; they hesitate, stagger under the federal fire, waver and are repulsed. Charge follows charge in rapid order, unparalleled salvos of artillery, drifts of shot and shell, whirlwinds of Minie bullets, continuous and destructive; the field is gory, and the air is thick with the breath of the dying. Three long days the battle rages, but the Flag of the union is triumphant, its stars shine brightly, and night brings victory.

In the beautiful cemetry where now quietly rest the dead of that terrible strife, lie the remains of over two hundred Michigan men, the third largest in number, and the largest in proportion to population.

"Sleep well, O sad-browed city,
  Whatever may betide;
Not under a nation's pity,
  But 'mid a nation's pride.
The vines that round you clamber,
  The brightest shall be, and best;
You sleep in the honor-chamber,
  Each one is a royal guest."

Benjamin F. Taylor thus beautifully describes the brilliant charge and the advance of the Flag up Mission Ridge, where several Michigan regiments were engaged, and bore a conspicuous part, while some of their Flags are claimed to have been the first to reach the summit:

"They dash out a little and then slacken; they creep up the mountain hand over hand, loading and firing, and wavering and halting, from the first line of works to the second.

"They burst into a charge with a cheer, and go over it. Sheets of flame baptize them; plunging shot tear away comrades on the right and left. It is no longer shoulder to shoulder; it is God for us all.

"Under tree trunks, among rocks, stumbling over the dead, struggling with the living, facing the steady fire of eight thousand infantry poured down upon their heads as if it were the old historic curse from heaven, they wrestle with the Ridge. Ten, fifteen, twenty minutes go by like a reluctant century. The hill sways up like a wall before them at an angle of forty-five degrees; but our brave mountaineers are clambering steadily on. They seem to be spurning the dull earth under their feet, and going up to do Homeric battle with the greater gods.

"If you look, you shall see, too, that these thirteen thousand are not a rushing herd of human creatures; that along the Gothic ridge a row of inverted V's is slowly moving up almost in line. At the angles is something that glitters like a wing,—the regimental Flag; and glancing along the front, you count fifteen of these colors that were borne at Pea Ridge, waved at Pittsburgh Landing, glorified at Stone River, riddled at Chickamauga,—up move the banners, now fluttering like a wounded bird, now faltering, now sinking out of sight. Three times the Flag of one regiment goes down. Do you know why? Just there lie three dead color sergeants. But the Flag, thank God, is immortal, and up it comes again, and the V's move on.

"The sun is not more than a hand's breadth from the edge of the mountain. Its level rays bridge the valley from Chattanooga to the ridge with beams of gold. It shines in the rebel faces; it brings out the national blue; it touches up the Flags. Oh! for the voice that could bid that sun to stand still.

Swarms of bullets sweep the hill; you can count twenty-eight bullets in one little tree. The rebels tumble rocks upon the rising line, they light the fuses and roll shells down the steep, they load the guns with handfuls of cartridges in their haste.

Just as the sun, weary of the scene, was sinking out of sight, the advance surged over the crest with magnificent bursts all along the line, exactly as you have seen the crested waves leap up at the breakwater. In a minute those Flags fluttered along the fringe, where fifty rebel guns were kenneled, *what* colors were the first on the mountain battlement one dare not try to say, bright honor itself might be proud to *bear*, nay to follow the hindmost. Foot by foot they had fought up the steep, slippery with much blood; let them go to glory together."

"'Their bugles sang truce for the night cloud had lowered,
And the sentinel stars set their watch in the sky;
And thousands had sunk on the ground overpowered,
The weary to sleep, and the wounded to die.'"

In the navy the Flag has been defended and honored, and conspicuously so in the brilliant victory of the Kearsarge over the Alabama, in a distant sea, in view of the people of a foreign nation, who watched with intense interest the most famous naval engagement of modern times.

The casualties were only one killed, and two wounded, in this gallant victory, yet the life's blood of a son of Michigan,—William Gouin of Detroit,—sealed the record of that glorious achievement.

Of the services of Michigan men in the navy during the war, there is unfortunately but little known, but undoubtedly they were there at their posts, distinguished officers and brave men, under the Flag of their country, with Foote, Dupont, Porter, and Farragut.

At a very early date, according to the voyagers and discoverers, the North American Indians, including those living on what is now known as the Peninsula of Michigan, made use of poles dressed with the wing of the Eagle and various colored cloths, and skins, as Flags, and many other emblems and devices were adopted by them to express their ideas of past and coming events, and as designating tribes one from another, as well as standards under which to rally in their conflicts with enemies.

At the Falls of St. Mary's, in 1671, representatives of the Indian tribes from the St. Lawrence, the Mississippi, the Lakes, and even the Red River, met in convention, and veteran officers from the armies of France, intermingled here and there with a Jesuit missionary, a cross having been raised and also a cedar post, on which the French lilies were inscribed, intended as a substitute for a Flag,—the first symbol of government established on Michigan territory. The representatives of the savage hordes were then informed that they were under the protection of the French King, and the lands were formally taken possession of by M. de Lusson, on behalf of his government.

While a detachment of English troops was advancing to occupy the fort at Detroit under the capitulation of 1760, a very singular symbol was made use of by the French officer in charge. Being indisposed to give up possession, he determined on resistance, and with this in view, he collected a body of Indians to assist him. Being aware that the Indians were liable to be strongly influenced by symbols, he erected a pole, placing thereon the image of a man's head, and on this he put a crow, telling the Indians that the head represented the English, and the crow himself, meaning that the French would scratch out the brains of the English. They did not believe him, however, but were of the opinion that the reverse would be the case. When the French officer gave up the fort the Indians loudly shouted in derision, and rejoiced that their prophecy had been verified.

It has been well established that no part of the United States has been under so many national standards as Michigan, having been governed by three different sovereignties, and five times its Flag has been changed. It was under the Flag of France from 1622 until 1760; that of England from 1760 until 1796. In that year the stars and stripes were raised at Detroit, by Captain Porter, with a detachment of General Wayne's army, the first American Flag that ever floated over Michigan. In the surrender of Hull at Detroit, in 1812, the standard of England was again established. In 1813, the victory of Commodore Perry, on Lake Erie, resulted in restoring Michigan to the union, and the star spangled banner floated once more on her shores and lakes.

It appears that, on the 22d of February, 1837, Stevens T. Mason, first Governor of Michigan, presented to the "Brady Guard" of Detroit, then in command of Capt. Isaac S. Rowland, a Flag, now in possession of the State, having on one side the devices and inscriptions on the seal of the State, with a Brady Guard and lady, and on the reverse, his own portrait. This was without doubt the first Flag bearing the State coat of arms, and was carried by the first uniformed company of militia in the State, having been organized April 13th, 1836, and was called into the service of the United States in the winter of 1837 as a frontier guard, during what is known as the "Patriot War," a very feeble and limited attempt at a Canadian revolution.

From that time forth, numerous Flags and banners had been in use, on which were placed the State arms, with various designs and emblems, but not until 1865 had there been adopted an official Flag of the State. This Flag, a combination of the State and national arms, recommended by John Robertson, Adjutant General, approved by Governor Henry H. Crapo, by whose order it was made in Philadelphia, in June of that year, was first unfurled on the occasion of the laying of the corner stone of the monument in the Soldiers' National Cemetery at Gettysburg, on the 4th of July, 1865. It is now the recognized standard of Michigan, and is carried by the State regiments, side by side with the stars and stripes.

The Flag is made up on one side, of the State arms, on a blue field with the appropriate and truthful inscription: "*Si quæris peninsulam, amœnam circumspice,*"—"If you seek a pleasant peninsula, look around you,"—a proud proclamation and implied challenge, and with the significant motto on the shield, "*Tuebor,*"—"I will defend,"—a gallant declaration, happily conceived, as an honest pledge, to guard and defend our border State, faithfully kept. On the reverse side, the arms of the United States, with the motto "*E Pluribus Unum.*"

There does not appear to have been any translation of the Latin inscriptions in the description of the seal recorded at the time it was presented to the constitutional convention adopting it, nor afterwards, at least no record of it can be found, yet members of that convention who have been questioned, agree as to the foregoing being the accepted rendering at the time of its adoption, and some of the very best authorities, who have been personally consulted, give the same translation. It is therefore deemed te be correct.

The many homogeneous designs, including nondescript animals, placed on flags, as the State coat of arms, and in daily use, in various other ways, even on State documents, few of them agreeing with the description of the great seal of the State, together with the differences made in rendering in English the Latin inscriptions thereon, have made it difficult to arrive at what really constitutes the State arms.

The design given in the following official description, as taken from the journal of the Constitutional Convention, will of course be accepted as correct:

DETROIT, *June 24th, 1835.*

To the Secretary of the Territory of Michigan:

In conformity with the following clause in the constitution, adopted by the convention now in session, I transmit you the within description and accompanying device for deposit in your office, hereby certifying that they are the papers to which reference is made in said clause, viz.:

'A great seal for the State shall be provided by the Governor, which shall contain the device and inscriptions represented and described in the papers relating thereto, signed by the president of the convention, and deposited in the office of the Secretary of the Territory.'

(Signed) JOHN BIDDLE,
President of the Convention.

DESCRIPTION OF THE GREAT SEAL OF THE STATE OF MICHIGAN.

A shield shall be represented on which shall be exhibited a peninsula extending into a lake, with the sun rising, and a man standing on the peninsula, with a gun in his hand.

On the top of the shield will be the word *Tuebor*, and underneath in a scroll will be the words, *Si quæris peninsulam, amœnam circumspice.*

There will be a supporter on each side of the shield, one of which will represent a moose, and the other an elk. Over the whole as a crest, will be the eagle of the United States, with the motto, "*E pluribus unum.*" Around will be the words, Great seal of the State of Michigan, A. D. MDCCCXXXV.

The American Moose, or Moose Deer,—the elk of Europe,—

is the largest of the deer kind, being taller than the horse. It is called by the Indians the Wampoose. The body is round, very compact and short; the head narrow, and clumsily shaped, and about two feet long, large protruding lips, the eye small, ears long, the neck and withers covered with a heavy coarse mane, tail not more than four inches in length, the legs, though very long are remarkably clean and firm. The whole body weighing from seven to twelve hundred pounds, is covered with hair of a grayish brown, coarse and angular, breaking if bent. Its movements are rather heavy; it does not gallop, but shuffles or ambles along, its joints cracking at every step, with a sound heard at some distance. It might seem from this description that the Moose was an uncouth and unsightly animal, yet when seen dashing through its native forests, it is said to produce on the mind of the beholder a feeling of beauty and sublimity. It is chiefly distinguished by its wide spreading palmated horns, entirely webbed like the foot of a duck. They are of great size, being two or three feet long, and sometimes four or five in the largest, weighing fifty or sixty pounds. They are shed annually in November. It feeds the same as the common deer, and in winter subsists on buds and barks of trees, and eats mosses dug from under the snow. It is long lived, and does not attain full growth until fourteen years of age. It was formerly common in all northern Europe and Asia, but is now rarely met with, and only in the extreme northern regions. When the United States were first settled by the whites it was found from the Carolinas to the polar regions; it is never seen now except in northern latitudes. It was believed by the ancients to graze walking backwards, and to have frequent attacks of epilepsy, and on that account was called by the Teutonic name of *Eland—miserable.* It had the reputation, especially of the fore hoofs, as a specific against disease, and as a remedy for its own disorder it was said to be obliged to smell its hoof before it could recover.

"The Elk of America, the Wapiti, is a large and noble species resembling the red deer of Europe; it has tall, round, branching horns, sometimes six feet high; the color is yellowish brown, the tail short, the form stately, the air majestic. Its length is seven to eight feet, its height four and a half to five. Its horns are shed in February or March. This animal is common in the Northwestern States, and thence north to Lake Winnepeg."

It is conceded that General Lewis Cass was the designer of the seal, and he seems to have been recognized as such by the convention, in the adoption of the following, on the 22d of June, prior to its final acceptance:

Resolved, That the President of this Convention tender to the Hon. Lewis Cass the thanks of this Convention, representing the people of Michigan, for the handsome State seal, presented by him to the State.

With a view of bringing about some uniformity in its use, on Flags, and in many other ways, where it may be found necessary to use it, it has been deemed advisable to enter thus fully into an investigation, and to fix, as far as possible, a definite understanding of the subject. For the purpose of aiding in this, the following letters are introduced:

KALAMAZOO, February 3d, 1877.

DEAR GENERAL:—Your letter of the 26th January last was received here during my absence, else would have been answered more promptly. I was a member (as you state) of the Michigan Constitutional Convention of 1835, and remember that Gen. Lewis Cass, then Secretary of War, presented to the people of Michigan, through John Biddle, the President of the convention, a device and motto to constitute the Seal of Michigan when we became a State. This device with the inscription was promptly and unanimously adopted by the convention. I was not an accomplished Latin scholar, but with some knowledge of the language, I construed the motto "*Si quœris peninsulam, amœnam circumspice*" to mean literally "If you seek a pleasant peninsula, look about you," and in the limited talk that was indulged in debate on the subject, I remember that Gen. Isaac E. Crary, Judge Ross Wilkins, and possibly others, gave the above as the literal translation of the motto, and they all agreed that this could not be improved by any attempt to make this translation more liberal. The word "*Tuebor*" was construed "I will defend," and if it had been placed on the seal and presented to the convention by some one not possessing the well earned popularity of Gen. Cass, would have been stricken out as savoring too much of pretentious vaunting; as it was, we all deferred to his superior judgment, and adopted the seal as it came from him.

As one of the citizens of Michigan, permit me to thank you for your efforts in making up a perfect record of the Flags to be placed in the new Capitol of Michigan, there to remain as part of the evidence that the people of the Peninsular State have done their full part in the preservation of the union.

Very respectfully

Your friend and obedient servant,

H. G. WELLS.

GEN'L JNO. ROBERTSON.

DETROIT, *February 6th, 1877.*

MY DEAR GENERAL:—In reply to your inquiry as to my recollections, if any, as to the origin of our State coat of arms, I can say that when a law student with Major Lewis Cass, in the year 1841, we had some conversation on the subject; and as I now recall it, he then stated, that when the matter was under consideration by the State authorities, his father, the late General Cass, was consulted, and together they selected and modified the celebrated inscription upon the black marble slab that marks the tomb of Sir Christopher Wren in the crypt of St. Paul's Cathedral, of which he was the distinguished architect. That inscription read, and still reads, as you know, thus: "*Si monumentum requiris circumspice*" ("if you require a monument (for me) look around you"). That is to say, my monument is the great temple itself which I have here designed and reared. Observing as the distinguishing feature of the State its peninsula character, they modified this motto by substituting *quaeris peninsulam amœnam* for the words *monumentum requiris;* so that the motto as shaped by them, then read as translated,—"If you seek a pleasant peninsula, look around you." This is the origin and history of this part of the motto, and it is all there is of it.

The word "*Tuebor*" ("I will defend") has reference to the frontier position of the State of Michigan. She lies close to the British territory, and on her devolves the defense not only of her soil, but also of the States south and east and west of her. She is the northern guard of the Union, and she says upon the shield, "*I will defend*" the frontier against all ene mies. In this view the word has a beautiful and brave signifi cance, and should never be changed while our position is thus in the fore front of exposure.

The eagle over the top of the coat of arms evidently symbolizes the superior authority and jurisdiction of the United States, to which authority our State has ever proved herself truly loyal.

I am glad to know that you are putting into pamphlet form the record of the Flag's history, and trust that the colors of the Union and those of the Peninsula State will always in the future, as in the past, be joined, peacefully blending with each other, and may God long preserve this Commonwealth, and the union of the States.

Truly yours,
D. BETHUNE DUFFIELD.

GENERAL JOHN ROBERTSON.

TECUMSEH, *January 27, 1877.*

DEAR GENERAL:—Yours of yesterday as to the adoption of the Michigan State coat of arms by the Constitutional Convention of 1835, was received this morning. I reply with pleasure, and will say a word or two as to the situation of affairs at the time of its adoption. I have heard of late some persons criticising the mottoes of the State coat of arms, say that "*Peninsulam amœnam*" should have been in the plural, so as to include both peninsulas, and amongst them, at a University commencement dinner a few years ago, one who I believe was a graduate of the University, and at any rate had held an important State office. But if they look back at the act of Congress of January 11, 1805, providing for the organization of the Territory of Michigan, and fixing its boundaries, and which remained the same as then established, so long as Michigan was a Territory, except as to the ten mile strip added on the north to the Territory of Indiana in 1816, when it was admitted into the union as a State, they might have seen or known that at the time of the sitting of the Constitutional Convention in 1835, there was no claim, or anticipated claim, to any lands west of the line drawn from the northern extremity of Lake Michigan to the national boundary in Lake Superior, nor was there then desired or asked for by the Convention, or by any one else, any such addition to our boundaries as is now embraced in what is known as the Upper Peninsula. It was an after thought of Congress to compensate Michigan, as it were, for the land on our southern boundary taken from us and added to the State of Ohio, a year or more after the sitting of the Convention, and the adoption of the State constitution and the State coat of arms. About the only voice raised in Congress against the robbery on our southern border was that of the venerable ex-President J. Q. Adams, then a member of the House of Representatives. But what could a young and weak Territory, with no voice in Congress but that of a delegate without a vote, do against a powerful State with some nineteen votes?

The literal English of "*Tuebor*" is: "I will defend." It means somewhat as if we would say, "We will defend even unto killing—unto death." "*Si quæris peninsulam, amœnam circumspice,*" literally translated is: "If you seek a pleasant peninsula, look around," or thus: "If you are looking for, or in search of a beautiful peninsula, look around you,—here it is."

Yours truly,

JOHN J. ADAM.

GEN'L JOHN ROBERTSON.

In the war with Mexico, Michigan maintained her Flag with honor, having in the service four companies in the 15th regular infantry, a regiment of volunteer infantry, and a company known as McReynolds' company of the 3d United States dragoons,—all doing good service, although the latter became conspicusly distinguished in the celebrated charge of Captain Phil. Kearney, on the Garetta of San Antonio, in the capture of the City of Mexico, on the 20th of August, 1847.

At Monroe, on the 4th of July, 1872, a celebration was held on the river Raisin battle ground, by survivors of the war of 1812, assembled from all parts of the country, when they displayed the Flag that they carried and defended at Fort Meigs. They had also with them a cannon captured from the enemy in 1813. They partook of a grand banquet, where toasts were given, and letters read from absent veterans, and others. They were in excellent spirits, although their ages ranged from eighty to one hundred years. Over fifteen thousand people were reported as present, and entering into the spirit of the day with great enthusiasm.

In the centennial year, Michigan, ably represented by her Governor and Board of Centennial Managers, evinced a pronounced and enlarged degree of patriotism, contributing a respectable and interesting share, to aid in making the "International Exhibition" an occasion worthy of a great nation; and prominently noticeable was the beautiful State building, together with her military displays, both of which were strikingly attractive.

On the great Independence Day, when were gathered together in Philadelphia multitudes of American citizens, and people from almost every other nation, assembled to honor the centennial national birth-day of America, State troops, under the Flag of Michigan, accompanied by Governor Bagley and staff, creditably represented their State.

Prominent among the wars of the past, looms up the great American rebellion. It stands out unique and extraordinary in all its aspects, viewed either in its immense proportions, the alacrity with which the forces on both sides were rushed into the field, as if by magic, the energy and skill with which it was prosecuted, the complete revolution in ships, arms, and munitions of war which it inaugurated, or the great result arrived at.

It was a fearful stake put up to settle grievances, merely domestic, and its recital forms a most remarkable page in the world's history. Aside from its magnitude, and its persistent and sanguinary course, prolonged from year to year, it was characterized by family as well as sectional hatred and strife, communities having a common interest and origin, with the blood of our patriot fathers coursing in their veins, met on the same field in deadly combat, families divided, parents and children against each other, brother against brother, ministers and people fighting and praying for each others' destruction, and a recent peaceful land was convulsed in civil war.

While indecision is characterizing the government at Washington, patriotism, and stern determination to settle the quarrel by the bayonet, were arousing the people of Michigan, and of the entire north.

Governor Wisner, in his outgoing message of January, 1861, to the Legislature, says, with characteristic firmness, "This is no time for vacilating councils when the cry of treason is ringing in our ears. The constitution as our fathers made it, is good enough for us, and must be enforced upon every foot of American soil."

Governor Blair, in his inaugural delivered at the same time, speaks for the State, and says: "In such a contest the god of battles has no attribute that can take sides with the revolutionists. Oh! for the firm, steady hand of a Washington or a Jackson to guide the Ship of State in this perilous time. Let us hope we shall find him on the fourth of March next. Meantime, let us abide in the faith of our fathers,—Liberty and Union, one and inseparable, now and forever!"

Stand by the Flag, on land and on sea, was the motto of the women of Michigan, inspiring and scattering patriotism amongst the people, and in the ranks at the front. Never doubting, always hopeful, ever confident of success, trusting in God's help for the cause of liberty, humanity, and right, while their interest in behalf of the soldier was intense and their industry for his benefit continuous.

Stand by the Flag, on land and on sea, were the watchwords of the men of Michigan. Their means, their sons, and their influence, were freely given to protect the Flag and maintain the Union.

On one occasion during the feudal times in Scotland, when chief met chief in battle array, two chiefs, with their adherents, were in one of the glens of that mountainous country, engaged in mortal combat, hand to hand and foot to foot, with *claymore* and *skein dhu*. One of them becoming much worsted, excited the fealty of one of his clan, a very old highlander, who stood on a projecting crag, in the face of the mountain, watching the contest with intense interest, too old to fight; he was merely a looker-on. He had several sons engaged for his chief. One falling by the hand of an opponent, the old man shouted in his Celtic tongue, "*Another son for the chief!*" And as one after another of his sons fell, he continued the shout, "*Another son for the chief!*" and again "*Another son for the chief!*" until the last had fallen. Then, quickly drawing the broad sword of his fathers from its rusted scabbard, he shouted with all the energy and enthusiasm of a true highlander "*Myself for the chief!*" and rushing down the mountain side into the affray, was soon cut down, and lay with his gallant sons in a gory bed.

So it was in many instances in Michigan during our recent war. Son after son went to the field, until all had gone, and one after another fell for the Union. Then the old father, in his agony of grief, with desperate loyalty and true patriotism in his heart, giving up all, family, friends, and home, rushes to the front shouting, *Myself for the Union!*

Hurriedly the advance of the Michigan contingent took up their line of march southward to defend the capital and protect the Flag, and as their many friends, with warm and true hearts, grasped the hand and kissed the brow, with "God bless and protect you," in affectionate whispers, thought reached not so far into the future, nor mind conceived that the little band then bidding adieu to loved ones and homes, were but the "*advance guard*" of the large army that was to follow, and which in saving the *national life*, and in bringing so much honor to the State, was to give up to the sword, the bayonet, and the bullet so much of life's best blood.

"We struck our camp at break of day, we marched unto the fight;
We laid the rose of pleasure down, and grasped the thorns of right;
The drum's tones were joy to us, the fife was sweetly shrill,
The flapping of our country's Flag—it made our pulses thrill."

Reaching Washington at a critical time, when Confederate troops flaunted their Flag on Arlington Heights, claiming defiantly, equality with the old banner of freedom floating from the dome of the National Capital, when rebel pickets patrolled the banks of the Potomac, and bivouacked under the old trees that shade the tomb of Washington.

This "Contingent" mustered into the service and left the State for the "front," in the order named, and at the dates given:

REGIMENTS.	Mustered In.		Left the State.	Mustered Out.		Returned to State.	
	Date.	Place.		Date.	Place.	Date.	Place.
1st Eng. & Mech.,	Oct. 29, 1861,	Marshall,	Dec. 17, '61	Sept. 22, '65	Nashville, Tenn.,	Sept. 26, '65	Jackson, Mich.
1st Cavalry,	Sept. 13, '61,	Detroit,	Sept. 29, '61	Mar. 10, '66	Salt Lake City, Utah,	P'd & disb'd	at Salt L. City.
2d "	Oct. 2, 1861,	Gd. Rapids,	Nov. 14, '61	Aug. 17, '65	Macon, Ga.,	Aug. 26, '65	Jackson, Mich.
3d "	Nov. 1, 1861,	"	Nov. 28, '61	Feb. 12, '66	San Antonio, Texas,	Mar. 10, '66	" "
4th "	Aug. 29, '62,	Detroit,	Sept. 26, '62	July 1, 1865	Nashville, Tenn.,	July 10, '65	Detroit, "
5th "	Aug. 30, '62,	"	Dec. 4, 1862	June 22, '65	Ft. Leavenworth, Ka.	July 1, 1865	" "
6th "	Oct. 13, 1862,	Gd. Rapids,	Dec. 10, '62	Nov. 24, '65	" " "	Nov. 30, '65	Jackson, "
7th "	Jan. 16, 1863,	"	Feb. 20, '63	Dec. 15, '65	" " "	Dec. 20, '65	" "
8th "	May 2, 1863,	Mt. Clemens,	May, 1863	Sept. 22, '65	Nashville, Tenn.,	Sept. 22, '65	" "
9th "	May 19, 1863,	Coldwater,	May 20, '63	July 21, '64	Lexington, N. C.,	July 30, '65	Detroit, "
10th "	Nov. 18, '63,	Gd. Rapids,	Dec. 1, 1863	Nov. 11, '65	Memphis, Tenn.,	Nov. 15, '65	Jackson, "
11th "	Dec. 10, '63,	Kalamazoo,	Dec. 17, '63	June 16, '65	Knoxville, Tenn.,	Sept. 28, '65	" "
1st Lt. Artil'ry, A,	May 28, 1861,	Coldwater,	June 1, '61	July 28, '65	Jackson, Mich.,	July 12, '65	" "
" " B,	Nov. 26, '61,	Gd. Rapids,	Dec. 17, '61	June 14, '65	Detroit, Mich.,	June 6, '65	Detroit, "
" " C,	Nov. 28, '61,	"	Dec. 17, '61	June 22, '65	" "	June 13, '65	" "
" " D,	Sept. 17, '61,	Wh'te Pig'on	Dec. 9, 1861	Aug. 3, 1865	Jackson, Mich.,	July 22, '65	Jackson, "
" " E,	Dec. 6, 1861,	Marshall,	Dec. 17, '61	July 30, '65	" "	July 16, '65	" "
" " F,	Jan. 9, 1862,	Coldwater,	March 3, '62	July 1, 1865	" "	June 24, '65	" "
" " G,	Jan. 17, 1862,	Kalamazoo,	Feb. 12, '62	Aug. 6, '65	" "	Aug. 2, '65	" "
" " H,	Mar. 6, 1862,	Monroe,	Mar. 13, '62	July 22, '65	" "	July 4, 1865	" "
" " I,	Aug. 29, '62,	Detroit,	Dec. 4, 1862	July 14, '65	Detroit, "	July 6, 1865	Detroit, "
" " K,	Feb. 20, '63,	Gd. Rapids,	Feb'y, 1863	July 22, '65	" "	July 12, '65	" "
" " L,	April 16, '63,	Coldwater,	May, 1863	Aug. 22, '65	Jackson, "	Aug. 19, '65	Jackson, "
" " M,	June 30, '63,	Mt. Clemens,	July, 1863	Aug. 1, '65	" "	July 12, '65	" "

13th Battery	Jan. 28, 1864,	Gd. Rapids,	Feb. 3, 1864	July 1, 1865	Jackson, Mich.,	June 22, '65	Jackson, Mich.
14th "	Jan. 5, 1864,	Kalamazoo,	Feb. 1, 1864	July 1, 1865	" "	June 21, '65	" "
Merrill Horse, H,	Sept. 6, 1861,	Fayette, Mo.,	Sept. 3, '61	Sept. 21, '65	Nashville, Tenn.,	P'd& disban	'd at Nashville.
" I,	Sept. 6, 1861,	" "	Sept. 3, '61	Sept. 21, '65	" "	" "	" "
" L,	Jan. 1, 1863,			Sept. 21, '65	" "	" "	" "
1st U. S. S. S. Co. C,	Aug. 26, '61,	Detroit,				" "	in the field.
" " I,	Mar. 4, 1862,	"				" "	" "
" " K,	Mar. 20, '62,	"	Mar. 27, '62			" "	" "
2d U. S. S. S. Co. B,	Oct. 4, 1861.	"				" "	" "
1st Inf., 3 mos.	May 1, 1861,	"	May 13, '61	Aug. 7, 1861	Detroit, Mich.,	Aug. 6, '61	Detroit, Mich.
" 3 years,	Sept. 16, '61,	Ann Arbor,	Sept. 16, '61	July 9, 1865	Jeffersonville, Ind.,	July 12, '65	Jackson, "
2d Infantry	May 25, 1861,	Detroit,	June 5, '61	July 28, '65	Delaney House, D. C.,	Aug. 1, '65	Detroit, "
3d "	June 10, '61,	Gd. Rapids,	June 13, '61	June 20, '64	Detroit, Mich.,	June 20, '64	" "
3d Inf., reorg'ized,	Oct. 15, 1864,	"	Oct. 20, '64	May 25, '66	Victoria, Texas,	June 10, '66	" "
4th Infantry	June 10, '61,	Adrian,	June 25, '61	June 28, '64	Detroit, Mich.,	June 26, '64	" "
4th Inf., reorg'z'd,	Oct. 14, 1864,	"	Oct. 22, '64	May 26, '66	Houston, Texas,	June 10, '66	" "
5th Infantry	Aug. 28, '61,	Detroit,	Sept. 11, '61	July 5, 1865	Jeffersonville, Ind.,	July 8, 1865	" "
6th H. A.,	Aug. 20, '61,	Kalamazoo,	Aug. 30, '61	Aug. 20, '65	New Orleans, La.,	Aug. 30, '65	Jackson, "
7th Infantry,	Aug. 22, '61,	Monroe,	Sept. 5, '61	July 5, 1865	Jeffersonville, Ind.,	July 7, 1865	" "
8th "	Sept. 23, '61,	Detroit,	Sept. 27, '61	July 30, '65	Delaney House, D. C.,	Aug. 3, '65	Detroit, "
9th "	Oct. 15, 1861,	"	Oct. 25, '61	Sept. 15, '65	Nashville, Tenn.,	Sept. 19, '65	Jackson, "
10th "	Feb. 6, 1862,	Flint,	Apr. 22, '62	July 19, '65	Louisville, Ky.,	July 22, '65	" "
11th "	Sept. 24, '61,	Wh'te Pig'on	Dec. 9, 1861	Sept. 30, '64	Sturgis, Mich.,	Sept. 25, '64	Sturgis, "
11th Inf., reorg'd,	Mar. 16, '65,	Jackson,	Mar. 18, '65	Sept. 16, '65	Nashville, Tenn.,	Sept. 23, '65	Jackson, "
12th Infantry,	Mar. 5, 1862,	Niles,	Mar. 18, '62	Feb. 15, '66	Little Rock, Ark.,	Feb. 27, '66	" "
13th "	Jan. 17, '62,	Kalamazoo,	Feb. 12, '62	July 25, '65	Louisville, Ky.,	July 27, '65	" "
14th "	Feb. 13, '62,	Ypsilanti,	Apr. 17, '62	July 18, '65	" "	July 21, '65	Detroit, "
15th "	Mar. 20, '62,	Monroe,	Mar. 27, '62	Aug. 13, '65	Little Rock, Ark.,	Sept. 1, '65	" "
16th "	Sept. 8, 1861,	Detroit,	Sept. 16, '61	July 8, 1865	Jeffersonville, Ind.,	July 12, '65	" "
17th "	Aug. 21, '62,	"	Aug. 27, '62	June 3, '65	Delaney House, D. C.,	June 7, '65	" "
18th "	Aug. 26, '62,	Hillsdale,	Sept. 4, '62	June 26, '65	Nashville, Tenn.,	July 2, 1865	Jackson, "
19th "	Sept. 25, '62,	Dowagiac,	Sept. 14, '62	June 10, '65	Washington, D. C.,	June 13, '65	Detroit, "

"CONTINGENT"—CONTINUED.

REGIMENTS.	Mustered In.		Left the State.	Mustered Out.		Returned to State.	
	Date.	Place.		Date.	Place.	Date.	Place.
20th Infantry,	Aug. 19, '62,	Jackson,	Sept. 1, '62	May 30, '65	Delaney House, D. C.,	June 4, '65	Jackson, Mich.
21st "	Sept. 4, 1862,	Ionia,	Sept. 12, '62	June 8, '62	Washington, D. C.,	June 13, '65	Detroit, "
22d "	Aug. 29, '62,	Pontiac,	Sept. 4, '62	June 26, '62	Nashville, Tenn.,	June 30, '65	' "
23d "	Sept. 13, '62,	E. Saginaw,	Sept. 18, '62	June 28, '62	Salisbury, N. C.,	July 7, 1865	" "
24th "	Aug. 15, '62,	Detroit,	Aug. 29, '62	June 30, '65	Detroit, Mich.,	June 20, '65	" "
25th "	Sept. 22, '62,	Kalamazoo,	Sept. 29, '62	June 24, '65	Salisbury, N. C.,	July 2, 1865	Jackson, "
26th "	Dec. 12, '62,	Jackson,	Dec. 13, '62	June 4, '65	Alexandria, Va.,	June 7, '65	" "
27th "	April 10, '63,	Ypsilanti,	Apr. 12, '63	July 26, '65	Delaney House, D. C.,	July 29, '65	Detroit, "
28th "	Nov. 10, '64,	Kalamazoo,	Oct. 26, '64	June 5, '65	Raleigh, N. C.,	June 8, '66	" "
29th "	Oct. 3, 1864,	Saginaw,	Oct. 6, '64	Sept. 6, '65	Murfreesboro, Tenn.,	Sept. 12, '65	" "
30th "	Jan. 9, 1865,	Detroit,	Didn't leave	June 30, '65	Detroit, Mich.,	P'd & disba	nded at Detroit.
1st S. S.,	July 7, 1863,	Dearborn,	July, 1863	July 28, '65	Delaney House, D. C.,	July 31, '65	Jackson, Mich.
102d U. S. C. T.,	Feb. 17, '64,	Detroit,	Mar. 28, '64	Sept. 30, '65	Charleston, S. C.,	Oct. 17, '65	Detroit, "

These regiments mostly carried Flags presented them by the people, some with the State Arms on one side, and with other devices on the reverse, while most of them had also the Flags which were furnished them by the U. S. Quartermaster Department, and all had full stands of colors given them by the government before their return to the State.

At the review of the Engineers and Mechanics, by Governor Blair and staff, at their camp near Marshall, on October 10, 1861, a very fine silk Flag was presented by Col. William P. Innis, to the regiment, in a very eloquent and appropriate speech by the Hon. F. W. Sherman, of Marshall, which was ably responded to in a very fitting manner by Lieut. Col. K. A. Hunton, in the absence of Colonel Innis.

The First Cavalry, while in Camp Lyon, near Detroit, on September 28, 1861, was made the recipients of a Flag from the citizens of Springwells. The presentation was made by the Hon. H. T. Backus, to which Col. T. F. Brodhead replied in a telling speech, full of burning eloquence and patriotism. The Flag was of blue silk, heavily fringed, with the national arms on each side, under which was emblazoned in gold letters, "First Michigan Cavalry."

In 1864 the citizens of Flint sent, by Colonel Minty, to the Fourth Cavalry a standard made of the heaviest blue banner silk with a gold colored fringe of heavy material. The State arms on the one side, on the reverse an eagle resting on a shield. Beneath the shield the motto of the regiment, "*In jure vincimus*,"—"We conquer in right." Inscribed on it battles of the regiment in beautiful letters. On an engraved silver plate on the staff "Presented to the 4th Regt. Mich. Cavalry by the friends of the Flint boys." "Blessings on our gallant Fourth. Victory o'er every foe."

While in the field in 1863, a Flag was procured and given to the Sixth Cavalry, by General James H. Kidd, of Ionia, then Major of the regiment. This Flag was borne through many battles, and is now in possession of the State. In the latter part of 1864, the citizens of Ionia had made a handsome silk Flag, which was delivered to the regiment through the Hon. James H. Kidd of that city. This Flag, after being carried to the close of the war, was taken with the regiment to Wyoming, on an expedition against the Indians, and was the first Flag that floated over Fort Reno, on Powder River. It is now in possession of General Kidd, and is a highly prized souvenir of the regiment.

The ladies of Mount Clemens gave to the Eighth Cavalry, a few days before it left for Kentucky, a valuable silk standard, with the name of the regiment finely written in gold. The presentation on their behalf was made by Robert P. Eldredge of that city, in a short but appropriate speech, to which Col. John Stockton, commanding the regiment, replied.

In 1863, and previous to leaving the State for the front, the ladies of Coldwater gave to the Ninth Cavalry a very neat and finely lettered silk standard, with the United States arms on one side, and on the other that of the State, with the inscription: "Presented by the ladies of Coldwater." The Flag passed through many hard battle-fields, but was carefully guarded and well defended.

On the afternoon of May 16, 1861, the ladies of Detroit presented to the First Infantry, on the Campus Martius, a silken Flag of very fine material. Addresses were made on behalf of the ladies, by the Hon. H. A. Morrow and D. Bethune Duffield, Esq., to which Colonel O. B. Wilcox, commanding the regiment, replied.

The ladies of Niles gave a National Color of silk to Company E of the Second Infantry before it left that city to join the regiment in Detroit, which afterwards became the regimental color. It was carried by the regiment through all its hard fought battles up to and including Fredericksburg, when it had become so tattered by wear, and some forty bullet holes, that it was deemed unserviceable, and was returned to the donors, who treasure it highly. It possesses a gallant record, having come out gloriously from every engagement, while eleven of its upholders or defenders were either killed or wounded.

On Monday, June 4, 1861, a delegation of thirty-four young ladies, representing the States of the union, arrayed in the colors of the national ensign, bearing a beautiful silk banner, arrived at cantonment Anderson, near Grand Rapids. On the Flag was the inscription in letters of gold: "Presented by the ladies of Grand Rapids to the Third Regiment Michigan Infantry." Colonel A. T. McReynolds delivered the presentation address in his well known eloquence, while the Chaplain of the regiment, Dr. Cummings, replied in a most appropriate manner.

On a beautiful spot of ground near the quarters of the Fourth Infantry, known as "Camp Williams," in the suburbs of the city of Adrian, on the 21st day of June, 1861, in the presence of thousands of people, the regiment in full dress was formed in a hollow square, inside of which Mrs. W. S. Wilcox, in behalf of the ladies of Adrian, in a few well chosen words, presented the command with an elegant regimental Flag. It was received by the men with cheers, and in their behalf was acknowledged in a brief but fitting speech by Col. D. A. Woodbury. Patriotic speeches were also made by C. M. Croswell, Esq., and Hon. Z. Chandler.

Previous to the leaving of the Fifth Infantry, in August, 1861, for the front, there was given to it at Fort Wayne, by Messrs. F. Buhl, Newland & Co., of Detroit, a National Color of fine silk and superb manufacture. Hon. Henry T. Backus addressed the regiment, who was replied to by Colonel H. D. Terry. This Flag was carried through the battles of the regiment. Under it some eight or ten color-bearers and guards were killed while defending it. On the return of the regiment to the State it was placed in possession of the "Regimental Association."

The citizens of Kalamazoo procured for the Sixth Infantry an elegant banner of the regulation standard. On a blue field were fine decorations in gold letters, and among the stars the single inscription: "Do your duty." The Flag was sent by the Hon. H. G. Wells to the regiment while in camp at Baltimore, where it was formally presented by Col. F. W. Curtenius, commanding. It was carried through the several battles of the regiment, and finally was sent to Kalamazoo, as the gift of the regiment, to Col. Curtenius.

A few weeks after the Seventh Infantry reached the front, and while it was stationed on the upper Potomac, near Leesburg, a stand of silk regulation colors was purchased and given to it by Colonel Grosvenor, commanding. On one of the stripes was inscribed the motto "*Tuebor*." In July, 1864, while in the field near Petersburg, Corporal Williams brought for the regiment a Flag of heavy blue silk, trimmed with gold fringe, presented by the ladies of Monroe, on which were embroidered the battles of the regiment. It was of rare beauty, and on it were also embroidered the State arms, with the motto "*Tuebor*" surmounted by an eagle with a scroll, on which was inscribed "Seventh Michigan Volunteers." Below the coat of arms was a double scroll with the inscription "Forlorn Hope" of Fredericksburg, Dec. 11, 1862," and underneath, "From the ladies of Monroe."

The reception of the Flag was acknowledged by the regiment in a set of resolutions, highly patriotic, and complimentary to the ladies. This color was carried with the others through the many battles of the Seventh, and was narrowly saved from capture in the Wilderness, by being taken from the staff and concealed by Colonel Lapoint under his clothing.

By a resolution of the regiment, it was given to Mrs. Colonel Grosvenor, as chairman of the body of ladies who presented it, and is now in her custody, highly prized by the entire community of Monroe.

In 1862, the citizens of Genesee county, through a committee composed of Hon. J. B. Walker, George T. Clark, and Chas. P. Avery, forwarded from Flint, to the Eighth infantry, for its gallant services, especially at the "Battle of Coosaw," a regimental Flag, rich and beautiful; the material of heavy silk, tasselled with gold. Embroidered on it were stars on the field, and "Eighth Regiment Michigan Infantry, One Country, One Destiny;" and which was afterwards adopted as the motto of the regiment. The staff surmounted with a gilt ball, on which rested an eagle in gold, with extended wings, a silver plate on the staff, with the inscription, "Presented to the officers and soldiers of the Eighth Regiment Michigan Infantry, by their friends and neighbors of Genesee county."

The colors reached the regiment at Beaufort, South Carolina, and were presented by General Isaac I. Stevens, commanding, in a very complimentary address, to which Colonel Fenton appropriately replied. He also sent a letter of thanks through the committee at Flint, to the donors throughout the county of Genesee.

The Rev. Dr. George Duffield, at Fort Wayne, in October, 1861, and shortly before the regiment left for the field, presented to the Ninth Infantry, in an eloquent address, breathing of true patriotism, a splendid, heavy silk banner, and inscribed thereon, in beautiful characters, "Presented on the 23d of October, 1861, by the Rev. George Duffield, of Detroit, Michigan, to the Ninth Michigan Infantry, his son, Col. W. W. Duffield, commanding."

"Thou hast given a banner to them that fear thee, that it may be displayed because of the truth. 'In the name of God will we set up our banners.'"

Hon. E. H. Thomson, in one of his eminently patriotic speeches, presented, on behalf of the citizens of Flint, a very elegant Flag made of the best roll silk, on which was inscribed the name of the regiment, and the word "*Tuebor;*" on a silver band on the staff the words, "Presented to the Tenth Regiment Michigan Infantry, by the citizens of Flint." A response, in good spirit and taste, by Colonel C. M. Lum, commanding the regiment, with a prayer by the Rev. J. S. Boyden. Judge Avery, of Flint, and Professor Siddons followed with brief and appropriate speeches.

A second Flag,—the gift of Colonel Charles M. Lum,—was given to the regiment immediately preceding the Atlanta campaign, which was carried through that campaign and the Sherman march to the sea.

The citizens of St. Joseph county, in December, 1861, while the regiment was in camp at White Pigeon, gave a handsome Flag to the Eleventh Infantry. A patriotic address was made by Mrs. J. W. Frey, of Three Rivers, with appropriate speeches by the Hon. J. E. Johnson and J. W. Frey, Esq., while replies were made in a fitting manner by Colonels W. L. Stoughton and W. J. May; also by Messrs. Samuel Chadwick and B. G. Bennett.

In 1862, on the ever memorable day, the 22d of February, the ladies of Niles gave to the Twelfth Regiment a valuable silk banner. It was presented on their behalf by Miss Mary Penrose, and a response made by the Colonel of the regiment, Francis Quinn.

While the Thirteenth Regiment was being recruited at Kalamazoo, the citizens, desirous of providing it with a set of colors, ordered them from New York through the Hon. G. H. Gale, but before their arrival the regiment had left for the front in Kentucky. When they were received, they were at once sent forward and presented, "*sans ceremonie,*" at Nashville, Tennessee, on dress parade, February 12, 1862. They were of elegant silk and fine workmanship, with the inscription in gold letters, "Presented by the citizens of Kalamazoo to the Thirteenth Michigan Infantry." When the regiment returned to Kalamazoo on veteran furlough, in February, 1864, the Flags were formally returned to the donors in an appropriate and earnest address, by Surgeon Foster Pratt, and were received on behalf of the village authorities by the Hon.

H. G. Wells. They have since been delivered in the care of the State for deposit with the other war Flags in the State Capitol.

These Flags were with the regiment in its severest battles,—baptized with fire at Perrysville, and in blood at Stone River, glorified at Mission Ridge, and riddled at Chickamauga, where three color bearers fell, and over fifty per cent of the regiment.

The ladies of Ypsilanti, in March, 1862, gave a Flag to the Fourteenth Regiment a short time before it left the State. On one side a figure of justice, by its side an eagle holding in its beak an American Flag, the folds of which were gracefully thrown around the figure. On a scroll is written in gold letters, "We came not to war on opinions, but to suppress treason."

The affair occurred at a review of the regiment by Governor Blair and staff. Professor J. M. B. Sill, on behalf of the ladies, in a characteristic speech, delivered the Flag, to which Colonel Robert P. Sinclair made an appropriate reply. In 1864 it was returned to the ladies by a committee of officers, selected by the regiment for that purpose.

On September 16, 1861, the ladies of Detroit, through Mrs. Charles H. Dunks, gave the Sixteenth, while in camp Backus, a superb Flag of the finest blue silk, inscribed thereon, "Stockton's Independent Regiment," with the State arms on one side, and on the reverse the arms of the United States, finely executed, on which was the motto, "Stand by the Union."

Hon. Ross Wilkins, of Detroit, in an address full of glowing patriotism, made the presentation, which was responded to by Colonel Stockton in a most appropriate style.

On the day the Eighteenth left its camp at Hillsdale, and while waiting at Toledo on the march to the front, an elegant Flag of the finest material and workmanship arrived by express, which had been ordered made by the Hon. Henry Waldron, who had been charged by the Governor with raising the regiment. It was presented by Mr. Waldron in one of his best speeches, to which an eloquent response was made by Major J. W. Horner, on behalf of the regiment, who assured the donor that it should never be dishonored while in their hands.

Soon after the Twentieth took the field, the ladies of Jackson gave it an elegant silk Flag, on which was inscribed the State arms. The Flag was sent to the regiment at Washington, but only reached it at the encampment opposite Fredericksburg. The presentation occurred on Thanksgiving Day, 1862, in a patriotic address by Mrs. Governor Blair, read by Assistant Surgeon O. P. Chubb, and an elegant response was made by Major Byron M. Cutcheon for the regiment. This Flag was carried in all the campaigns of the regiment until the spring of 1864, when becoming very much tattered and torn it became necessary to send it back to the State.

A beautiful silk Flag was provided by the ladies of Ionia and delivered to the Twenty-first Regiment, on the 6th of September, 1862, at that city. The center of the Flag decorated with the American eagle, holding its quiver of arrows, olive branch, etc. Over this a small national Flag, and beneath it the words "Union," "Constitution." An excellent speech was made by L. B. Soule, Esq., on behalf of the ladies, to which Colonel A. A. Stevens, commanding the regiment, appropriately replied. Afterwards speeches were made by Z. Chandler, T. W. Ferry, and F. W. Kellogg. At the same time there was presented a Flag by the children of the Grand Haven Sunday schools to company G of the regiment.

The Flag given the regiment was carried through all of its engagements, brought back to the State, and at a celebration on July 4, 1865, was formally returned, on behalf of the regiment, to the ladies by the Hon. John Avery, of Greenville, the highest ranking officer of the regiment present, and was received on behalf of the ladies by the Hon. John B. Hutchins, of Ionia.

On September 4, 1862, the Twenty-second Regiment was given a Flag just before leaving Pontiac, by the young ladies of that city. The presentation was made by J. S. Dewey, Esq., in a short but very eloquent address. Colonel Wisner, in the name of the regiment, received the Flag, in a brief but patriotic speech. While Mr. Dewey was addressing the regiment, the Flag was borne by two beautiful and accomplished young ladies,—Miss Emma Adams and Miss Julia Comstock.

This Flag was defended at Chickamauga in the heroic charge of the regiment, nobly, where three color bearers were killed and several wounded, with nearly the entire regiment killed, wounded, or prisoners.

In August, 1862, Messrs. F. Buhl, Newland & Co. gave the Twenty-fourth, on Campus Martius, Detroit, a very costly Flag, red, white, and blue in stars of raised work, inscribed on the Flag, "24th Michigan Infantry." D. E. Harbaugh, Esq., made a very appropriate presentation speech, to which Colonel Morrow made a very brief but patriotic reply. The Flag was carried through all the battles of the regiment up to Gettysburg, where, in upholding and saving it, four color bearers were killed and three wounded. It was then returned to the State, being so tattered and torn as to be unfit for service.

In 1865, the citizens of Detroit, through General Mark Flanigan, gave the regiment a superb silk Flag, elegantly embroidered with the Michigan and United States arms, together with the battles in which the regiment had participated. The Flag was taken to the regiment, then at Camp Butler, Illinois, by Major William Hutchinson, and presented, together with a letter from General Flanigan. Colonel A. M. Edwards, commanding the regiment, received it in an appropriate reply.

Before the Twenty-fifth left Kalamazoo for the front, a silk Flag was presented to the regiment by the Hon. H. G. Wells,

6

on behalf of the citizens of that place, and a response made by Colonel O. H. Moore, commanding. The Flag was of the regulation standard, with the inscription, "This Flag is given in faith that it will be carried where honor and duty leads." It was first given to the breeze at Green River, Kentucky, on the morning of July 4, 1863, where the regiment, with less than three hundred and fifty men, acquired an enviable reputation for a gallant defense,—repulsing the attack of John Morgan with three thousand men.

While the Twenty-sixth was in camp at Jackson, and immediately preceding the march of the regiment to the front, it received, at the fair hands of the ladies of Jackson, a magnificent silk Flag, the field of blue, with letters of gold. The presentation speech was made in good taste by the Hon. Fidus Livermore, who had been commissioned by the Governor as commandant of camp to raise the regiment, and which was responded to in a patriotic manner by Colonel J. S. Farrar, commanding. The Flag was borne by the regiment through many sanguinary fields, and what is left of it is now in the archives of the State.

The Twenty-seventh had a Flag prepared by the ladies of Port Huron and carried to Ypsilanti, where it was delivered on their behalf by the Hon. James Sanborn, of Port Huron, to which Colonel D. M. Fox replied for the regiment.

The Flag was of the first quality and superb workmanship.

To have been able to give the histories of regiments as the history of their respective Flags, would have been preferable, but brevity became a necessity, and the bare record of their engagements merely is given; yet, as it is read, and the stirring scenes and momentous results are recalled, associated with Stone River, Manassas, Antietam, Gettysburg, Chicamauga, Atlanta, Mission Ridge, Nashville, the Wilderness, Spottsylvania, and many of the other fields hereafter mentioned, the history of the Flag of Michigan cannot be forgotten.

The services of troops in war are generally estimated by their battles, and whether successful or otherwise, they so far establish the history of their colors. With this in view, are narrated the encounters of Michigan troops with the enemy in defense of the Union, and the "Old Flag," in all of which their Flags maintained a conspicuous position, and were gallantly defended, rendering the history of each interesting and glorious.

These encounters are taken from the official reports of commanders of regiments, varying in character and importance from a general engagement to an ordinary skirmish, and occurring at the places and dates as enumerated with each regiment.

ENGINEERS AND MECHANICS.—Mill Springs, Ky., January 19, 1862. Farmington, Miss., May 9, 1862. Siege of Corinth, May 10 to 31, 1862. Perrysville, Ky., October 8, 1862. Lavergne, Tenn., January 1, 1863. Chattanooga, Tenn., October 6, 1863. Siege of Atlanta, Ga., July 22 to September 2, 1864. Savannah, Ga., December 11 to 21, 1864. Bentonville, N. C., March 19, 1865.

FIRST CAVALRY.—Winchester, Va., March 23, 1862. Middletown, Va., March 25, 1862. Strasburg, Va., March 27, 1862. Harrisonburg, Va., April 22, 1862. Winchester, Va., May 24, 1862. Orange Court House, Va., June 16, 1862. Cedar Mountain, Va., August 9, 1862. Bull Run, second, Va., August 30, 1862. Occoquan, Va., February —, 1863. Thoroughfare Gap, Va., May 21, 1863. Greenwich, Va., May 30, 1863. Hanover, Va., June 30, 1863. Hunterstown, Penn., July 2, 1863. Gettysburg, Penn., July 3, 1863. Monterey, Md., July 4, 1863. Cavetown, Md., July 5, 1863. Smithtown, Md., July 6, 1863. Boonsboro, Md., July 6, 1863. Hagerstown, Md., July 6, 1863. Williamsport, Md., July 6, 1863. Boonsboro, Md., July 8, 1863. Hagerstown, Md., July 10, 1863. Williamsport, Md., July 10, 1863. Falling Waters, Md., July 14, 1863. Snicker's Gap, Va., July 19, 1863. Kelly's Ford, Va., September 13, 1863. Culpepper Court House, Va., September 14, 1863. Raccoon Ford, Va., September 16, 1863. White's Ford, Va., September 21, 1863. Jack's Shop, Va., September 26, 1863. James City, Va., October 12, 1863. Brandy Station, Va., October 13, 1863. Buckland's Mills, Va., October 19, 1863. Stevensburg, Va., November 19, 1863. Morton's Ford, Va., November 26, 1863. Richmond, Va., March 1, 1864. Wilderness, Va., May 6 and 7, 1864. Beaver Dam Station, Va., May 9, 1864. Yellow Tavern, Va., May 10 and 11, 1864. Meadow Bridge, Va., May 12, 1864. Milford, Va., May 27, 1864. Hawe's Shop, Va., May 28, 1864. Baltimore X Roads, Va., May 29, 1864. Coal Harbor, Va., May 30 and June 1, 1864. Travillian Station, Va., June 11 and 12, 1864. Coal Harbor, Va., July 21, 1864. Winchester, Va., August 11, 1864. Front Royal, Va., August 16, 1864. Leetown, Va., August 25, 1864. Shepardstown, Va., August 25, 1864. Smithfield, Va., August 29, 1864. Berryville, Va., September 3, 1864, Summitt, Va., September 4, 1864. Opequan, Va., September, 19, 1864. Winchester, Va., September 19, 1864. Luray, Va., September 24, 1864. Port Republic, Va., July 26, 27, and 28, 1864. Mount Crawford, Va., October 2, 1864. Woodstock, Va., October 9, 1864. Cedar Creek, Va., October 19, 1864. Madison Court House, Va., December 24, 1864. Louisa Court House, Va., March 8, 1865. Five Forks, Va., March 30, 31, and April 1, 1865. South Side R. R., Va., April 2, 1865. Duck Pond Mills, Va., April 4, 1865. Ridges, or Sailor's Creek, Va., April 6, 1865. Appomattox Court House, Va., April 8 and 9, 1865. Willow Springs, Dakota T., August 12, 1865.

Second Cavalry.—Point Pleasant, Mo., March 9, 1862. Tiptonville, Mo., March —, 1862. New Madrid, Mo., March 13, 1862. Island No. 10, Mo., March 14 to April 7th, 1862. Pine Hill, Miss., May 2, 1862. Monterey, Miss., May 3, 1862. Farmington, Miss., May 5, 1862. Siege of Corinth, Miss.,

May 10 to 30, 1862. Boonville, Miss., June 1, 1862. Blackland, Miss., June 5, 1862. Baldwin, Miss., June —, 1862. Boonville, Miss., July 1, 1862. Reinzie, Miss., August —, 1862. Perryville, Ky., October 8, 1862. Harodsburg, Ky., October 10, 1862. Lancaster, Ky., October 12, 1862. Rocastle River, Ky., October —, 1862. Estillville, Va., 1862. Blountsville, Tenn., 1862. Zollicoffer, Tenn., 1862. Watanaga, Tenn., 1862. Jonesville, Va., 1862. Bacon Creek, Ky., December 24, 1862. Glasgow, Ky., December —, 1862. Milton, Tenn., February 18, 1863. Cainesville, Tenn., February 19, 1863. Spring Hill, Tenn., February 29, 1863. Columbia, Tenn., March 4 and 5, 1863. Hillsboro, Tenn., March 12, 1863. Brontwood, Tenn., March 25, 1863. McGarvick's Ford, Tenn., April, 1863. Triune, Tenn., June 4, 1863. Rover, Tenn., June 23, 1863. Middletown, Tenn., June 24, 1863. Shelbyville, Tenn., June 27, 1863. Elk River Ford, Tenn., July 2, 1863. Dechard, Tenn., July 4, 1863. Chicamagua, Tenn., September 18, 19, and 20, 1863. Anderson X Roads, Tenn., October, 1863. Sparta, Tenn., December, 1863. Dandridge, Tenn., December 24, 1863. Mossy Creek, Tenn., December 29, 1863. Dandridge, Tenn., January 17, 1864. Pigeon River, Tenn., January 27, 1864. Dug Gap, Ga., May 13 and 14, 1864. Red Clay, Ga., May, 1864. Ettowa River, Ga., May 24, 26, 27, and 28, 1864. Ackworth, Tenn., June 2 and 5, 1864. Nashville, Tenn., August 30, 1864. Campbellsville, Tenn., September 5, 1864. Franklin, Tenn., September 27, 1864. Cypress River, Tenn., October 7, 1864. Raccoon Ford, Tenn., October 30, 1864. Shoal Creek, Tenn., November 5, 1864. Lawrenceburg, Tenn., November 21, 1864. Campbellsville, Tenn., November 24, 1864. Columbia, Tenn., November 25, 26, and 27, 1864. Spring Hill, Tenn., November 29, 1864. Bethesda Church, Tenn., November 29, 1864. Franklin, Tenn., November 30, 1864. Nashville, Tenn., December 15 and 16, 1864. Richland Creek, Tenn., December 24, 1864. Pulaski, Tenn., December 25, 1864. Sugar Creek, Tenn., December 26, 1864. Priceton Yard, Tenn., January 6, 1865. Corinth, Miss., February, 1865. Tuscaloosa, Ala., April 1, 1865. Trion, Ala., April 2, 1865. Bridgeville, Ala., April 6, 1865. Talladaga, Ala., April 23, 1865.

THIRD CAVALRY.—New Madrid, Mo., March 13, 1862. Siege of Island No. 10, Mo., March 14 to April 7, 1862. Farmington, Miss., May 5, 1862. Siege of Corinth, Miss., May 10 to 31, 1862. Spangler's Mills, Miss., July 26, 1862. Bay Springs, Miss., September 10, 1862. Iuka, Miss., September 19, 1862. Corinth, Miss., October 3 and 4, 1862. Hatchie, Miss., October 6, 1862. Holly Springs, Miss., November 7, 1862. Hudsonville, Miss., November 14, 1862. Lumkin's Mills, Miss., November 29, 1862. Oxford, Miss., December 2, 1862. Coffeeville, Miss., December 5, 1862. Brownsville, Miss., January 14, 1863. Clifton, Miss., February 10, 1863. Panola, Miss., July 20, 1863. Grenada, Miss., August 14, 1863. Byhalia, Miss., October 12, 1863. Wyatt's Ford, Miss., October 13, 1863. Ripley, Miss., November 29, 1863. Orizaba, Miss., November 30, 1863. Ellistown, Miss., December 3, 1863. Purdy, Miss., December 22, 1863. Jack's Creek, Miss., December 24, 1863.

FOURTH CAVALRY.—Stamford, Ky., October 14, 1862. Gallatin, Tenn., November 8, 1862. Lebanon, Tenn., November 9, 1862. Rural Hill, Tenn., November 15, 1862. Baird's Mill, Tenn., November 30, 1862. Hollow Tree Gap, Tenn., December 4, 1862. Wilson's Creek Road, Tenn., December 11, 1862. Franklin, Tenn., December 12, 1862. Rural Hill, Tenn., December 20, 1862. Wilson's Creek, Tenn., December 21, 1862. Lavergne, Tenn., December 26, 1862. Jefferson's Bridge, Tenn., December 27, 1862. Nashville Pike, Tenn., December 30, 1862. Stone River, Tenn., December 31, 1862. Lavergne, Tenn., January 1, 1863. Manchester Pike, Tenn., January 5, 1863. Harpeth River, Tenn., January 12, 1863.

Cumberland Shoals, Tenn., January 13, 1863. Bradyville, Tenn., January 21, 1863. Woodbury, Tenn., January 22, 1863. Rover, Tenn., January 31, 1863. Charlotte, Tenn., February 6, 1863. Rover, Tenn., February 13, 1863. Auburn, Tenn., February 19, 1863. Liberty, Tenn., February 20, 1863. Unionville, Tenn., March 4, 1863. Thompson's Station, Tenn., March 9, 1863. Rutherford Creek, Tenn., March 10, 1863. Duck River, Tenn., March 11, 1863. Prosperity Church, Tenn., April 2, 1863. Liberty, Tenn., April 3, 1863. Snow Hill, Tenn., April 4, 1863. McMinnville, Tenn., April 21, 1863. Statesville, Tenn., April 22, 1863. Alexandria, Tenn., April 23, 1863. Wartrace, Tenn., April 29, 1863. Middletown, Tenn., May 22, 1863. Wartrace, Tenn., June 3, 1863. Versailles, Tenn., June 10, 1862. Cherry Valley, Tenn., June 16, 1863. Shelbyville, Tenn., June 27, 1863. Hickory Creek, Tenn., July 4, 1863. Tullahoma, Tenn., July 5, 1863. Rock Island, Tenn., August 2, 1863. Sparta, Tenn., August 9, 1863. Sperry's Mill, Tenn., August 17, 1863. Smith's Cross Roads, Tenn., August 21, 1863. Reed's Bridge, Ga., September 18, 1863. Chickamauga, Tenn., September 19, 20, 21, 1863. Rossville, Ga., September 22, 1863. Cotton Port, Tenn., September 30, 1863. Smith's Cross Roads, Tenn., October 1, 1863. Hill Creek, Tenn., October 3, 1863. McMinnville, Tenn., October 4, 1863. Chattanooga, Tenn., November 17, 1863. Cleveland, Tenn., December 12, 1863. Mission Ridge, Tenn., November 25, 1863. Tunnel Hill, Ga., January 28, 1864. Farmer's Bridge, Ga., May 15, 1864. Arundel Creek, Ga., May 16, 1864. Kingston, Ga., May 18, 1864. Dallas, Ga., May 24, 1864. Villa Ricca, Ga., May 26, 1864. Lost Mountain, Ga., May 27, 1864. Big Shanty, Ga., June 9, 1864. McAffee's X Roads, Ga., June 11, 1864. Noonday Creek, Ga., June 19, 1864. Lattimer's Mills, Ga., June 20, 1864. Noonday Creek, Ga., June 23, 1864. Kenesaw Mountain, Ga., June 27, 1864. Rosswell, Ga., July 4, 1864. Lebanon Mills, Ga., July 14, 1864. Stone Mountain,

---

Ga., July 18, 1864. Covington, Ga., July 22, 1864. Flatt Rock, Ga., July 27, 1864. Flatt Rock, Ga., July 28, 1864. Siege of Atlanta, Ga., August 1 to 14, 1864. Fair Oaks, Ga., August 19, 1864. Jonesboro, Ga., August 19, 1864. Lovejoy's Station, Ga., August 20, 1864. McDonough's, Ga., August 20, 1864. Rosswell, Ga., September 26, 1864. Sweet Water, Ga., October 2, 1864. Moses Creek, Ga., October 3, 1864. Lost Mountain, Ga., October 5, 1864. New Hope Church, Ga., October 7, 1864. Stilesboro, Ga., October 11, 1864. Rome, Ga., October 12, 1864. Rome, Ga., October 12, 1864. Blue Pond, Ga., October 21, 1864. Selma, Ala., April 2, 1865. Double Bridges, Ga., April 18, 1865. Macon, Ga., April 20, 1865. Capture of Jeff. Davis, Ga., May 10, 1865.

FIFTH CAVALRY.—Hanover, Va., June 30, 1863. Hunterstown, Penn., July 2, 1863. Gettysburg, Penn., July 3, 1863. Monterey, Md., July 4, 1863. Cavetown, Md., July 5, 1863. Smithtown, Md., July 6, 1863. Boonsboro, Md., July 6, 1863. Hagerstown, Md., July 6, 1863. Williamsport, Md., July 6, 1863. Boonsboro, Md., July 8, 1863. Hagerstown, Md., July 10, 1863. Williamsport, Md., July 10, 1863. Falling Waters, Md., July 14, 1863. Snicker's Gap, Va., July 19, 1863. Kelly's Ford, Va., September 13, 1863. Culpepper Court House, Va., September 14, 1863. Raccoon Ford, Va., September 16, 1863. White's Ford, Va., September 21, 1863. Jack's Shop, Va., September 26, 1863. James City, Va., October 12, 1863. Brandy Station, Va., October 13, 1863. Buckland's Mills, Va., October 19, 1863. Stevensburg, Va., November 19, 1863. Morton's Ford, Va., Nov. 26, 1863. Richmond, Va., March 1, 1864. Wilderness, Va., May 6 and 7, 1864. Beaver Dam Station, Va., May 9, 1864. Yellow Tavern, Va., May 10, 11, 1864. Meadow Bridge, Va., May 12, 1864. Milford, Va., May 27, 1864. Hawes' Shop, Va., May 28, 1864. Baltimore X Roads, Va., May 29, 1864. Cold Harbor, Va., May 30, June 1, 1864. Travillian Station, Va., June 11, 12, 1864.

Cold Harbor, Va., July 21, 1864. Winchester, Va., August 11, 1864. Front Royal, Va., August 16, 1864. Leetown, Va., August 25, 1864. Shepardstown, Va., August 25, 1864. Smithfield, Va., August 29, 1864. Berryville, Va., September 3, 1864. Summitt, Va., September 4, 1864. Opequan, Va., September 19, 1864. Winchester, Va., September 19, 1864. Luray, Va., September 24, 1864. Port Republic, Va., July 26, 27, 28, 1864. Mount Crawford, Va., October 2, 1864. Woodstock, Va., October 9, 1864. Cedar Creek, Va., October 19, 1864. Newton, Va., November 12, 1864. Madison Court House, Va., December 24, 1864. Louisa Court House, Va., March 18, 1865. Five Forks, Va., March 30, 31, April 1, 1865. South Side R. R., Va., April 2, 1865. Duck Pond Mills, Va., April 4, 1864. Ridges, or Sailor's Creek, Va., April 6, 1865. Appomattox Court House, Va., April 8, 9, 1865.

SIXTH CAVALRY.—Hanover, Va., June 30, 1863. Hunterstown, Pa., July 2, 1863. Gettysburg, Pa., July 3, 1863. Monterey, Md., July 4, 1863. Cavetown, Md., July 5, 1863. Smithtown, Md., July 6, 1863. Boonsboro, Md., July 6, 1863. Hagerstown, Md., July 6, 1863. Williamsport, Md., July 6, 1863. Boonsboro, Md., July 8, 1863. Hagerstown, Md., July 10, 1863. Willamsport, Md., July 10, 1863. Falling Waters, Md., July 14, 1863. Snicker's Gap, Va., July 19, 1863. Kelly's Ford, Va., September 13, 1863. Culpepper Court House, Va., September 14, 1863. Raccoon Ford, Va., September 16, 1863. White's Ford, Va., September 21, 1863, Jack's Shop, Va., September 26, 1863. James City, Va., October 12, 1863. Brandy Station, Va., October 13, 1863. Buckland's Mills, Va., October 19, 1863. Stevensburg, Va., November 19, 1863, Morton's Ford, Va., November 26, 1863. Richmond, Va., March 1, 1864. Wilderness, Va., May 6, 7, 1864. Beaver Dam Station, Va., May 9, 1864. Yellow Tavern, Va., May 10, 11, 1864. Meadow Bridge, Va., May 12,

1864. Hanover, Va., May 27, 1864. Hawes' Shop, Va., May 28, 1864. Baltimore X Roads, Va. May 29, 1864. Cold Harbor, Va., May 30, June 1, 1864. Travillian Station, Va., June 11, 12, 1864. Cold Harbor, Va. July 21, 1864. Winchester, Va., August 11, 1864. Front Royal, Va., August 16, 1864. Leetown, Va., August 25, 1864. Shepardstown, Va., August 26, 1864. Smithfield, Va., August 29, 1864. Berryville, Va., September 3, 1864. Summit, Va., September 4, 1864. Opequan, Va., September 19, 1864. Winchester, Va., September 19, 1864. Luray, Va., September 24, 1864. Port Republic, Va., September 26, 27, 28, 1864. Mount Crawford, Va., October 2, 1864. Woodstock, Va., October 9, 1864. Cedar Creek, Va., October 19, 1864. Madison Court House, Va., December 24, 1864. Louisa Court House, Va., March 8, 1865. Five Forks, Va., March 30, 31, April 1, 1865. South Side R. R., Va., April 2, 1865. Duck Pond Mills, Va., April 4, 1865. Ridges, or Sailor's Creek, Va., April 6, 1865. Appomattox Court House, Va., April 6, 1865. Little Laramie, Dakota Ter., August 6, 1865.

SEVENTH CAVALRY.—Thoroughfare Gap, Va., May 21, 1863. Greenwich, Va., May 30, 1863. Hanover, Va., June 30, 1863. Hunterstown, Penn., July 2, 1863. Gettysburg, Penn., July 3, 1863. Monterey, Md., July 4, 1863. Cavetown, Md., July 5, 1863. Smithtown, Md., July 6, 1863. Boonsboro, Md., July 6, 1863. Hagarstown, Md., July 6, 1863. Williamsport, Md., July 6, 1863. Boonsboro, Md., July 8, 1863. Hagerstown, Md., July 10, 1863. Williamsport, Md., July 10, 1863. Falling Waters, Md., July 14, 1863. Snicker's Gap, Va., July 19, 1863. Kelly's Ford, Va., September 13, 1863. Culpepper Court House, Va., September 14, 1863. Raccoon Ford, Va., September 16, 1863. White's Ford, Va., September 21, 1863. Jack's Shop, Va., September 26, 1863. James City, Va., October 12, 1863. Brandy station, Va., October 13, 1863. Buckland's Mills, Va., October 19, 1863. Stevensburg, Va.,

November 19, 1863. Morton's Ford, Va., November 26, 1863. Richmond, Va., March 1, 1864. Wilderness, Va., May 6 and 7, 1864. Beaver Dam Station, Va., May 9, 1864. Yellow Tavern, Va., May 10 and 11, 1864. Meadow Bridge, Va., May 12, 1864. Milford, Va., May 27, 1864. Hawes' Shop, Va., May 28, 1864. Baltimore X Roads, Va., May 29, 1864. Cold Harbor, Va., May 30, and June 1, 1864. Travillian Station, Va., June 11 and 12, 1864. Cold Harbor, Va., July 21, 1864. Winchester, Va., August 11, 1864. Front Royal, Va., August 16, 1864. Leetown, Va., August 25, 1864. Shepardstown, Va., August 25, 1864. Smithfield, Va., August 29, 1864. Berryville, Va., September 3, 1864. Summitt, Va., September 4, 1864. Opequan, Va., September 19, 1864. Winchester, Va., September 19, 1864. Luray, Va., September 24, 1864. Port Republic, Va., September 26, 27, and 28, 1864. Mount Crawford, Va., October 2, 1864. Woodstock, Va., October 9, 1864. Cedar Creek, Va., October 19, 1864. Madison Court House, Va., December 24, 1864. Louisa Court House, Va., March 8, 1865. Five Forks, Va., March 30, 31, and April 1, 1865. South Side R. R., Va., April 2, 1865. Duck Pond Mills, Va., April 4, 1865. Ridges or Sailor's Creek, Va., April 6, 1865. Appomattox Court House, Va., April 8 and 9, 1865. Little Laramie, Dakota Ter., August 1, 1865.

EIGHTH CAVALRY.—Triplet Bridge, Ky., June 19, 1863. Lebanon, Ky., July 5, 1863. Laurenceburg, Ky., July 9, 1863. Salvica, Ky., July 10, 1863. Buffington's Island, O., July 19, 1863. Winchester, Ky., July 25, 1863. Salineville, O., July 26, 1863. Lancaster, Ky., July 30, 1863. Stamford, Ky., July 31, 1863. Kingston, Tenn., September 1, 1863. Cleveland, Tenn., September 18, 1863. Calhoun, Tenn., September 26, 1863. Athens, Tenn., September 27, 1863. Loudon, Tenn., September 29, 1863. Philadelphia, Tenn., October 23, 1863. Sweet Water, Tenn., October 26, 1863. Lenoir Station, Tenn., November 12, 1863. Campbell's Station,

Tenn., November 16, 1863. Knoxville, Tenn., November 18, 1863. Rutledge, Tenn., December 10, 1863. Reams' Station, Tenn., December 14, 1863. New Market, Tenn., December 25, 1863. Mossey Creek, Tenn., January 10, 1864. Dandridge, Tenn., January 17, 1864. Fair Garden, Tenn., January 24, 1864. Sevierville, Tenn., January 27, 1864. Kenesaw Mountain, Ga., July 1, 1864. Sweet Water, Ga., July 3, 1864. Chattahoochie, Ga., July 4, 1864. Moore's Ridge, Ga., July 12, 1864. Covington, Ga., July 28, 1864. Macon, Ga., July 30, 1864. Sunshine Church, Ga., July 31, 1864. Eatonton, Ga., August 1, 1864. Mulberry Creeek, Ga., August 3, 1864. Henryville, Tenn., November 23, 1864. Mount Pleasant, Tenn., November 24, 1864. Duck River, Tenn., November 24, 1864. Nashville, Tenn., December 14 to 22, 1864.

NINTH CAVALRY.—Triplet Bridge, Ky., June 24, 1863. Lebanon, Ky., July 5, 1863. Salvica, Ky., July 7, 1863. Cummings Ferry, Ky., July 9, 1863. Buffington's Island, Ohio, July 19, 1863. Salineville, Ohio, July 26, 1863. Loudon, Tenn., September 2, 1863. Cumberland Gap, Tenn., September 9, 1863. Carter's Station, Tenn., September 21, 1863. Zollicoffer, Tenn., September 25, 1863. Leesburg, Tenn., September 29, 1863. Blue Springs, Tenn., October 5 and 10, 1863. Rheatown, Tenn., October 11, 1863. Siege of Knoxville, Tenn., December 5, 1863. Morristown, Tenn., December 10, 1863. Russellville, Tenn., December 12, 1863. Beans, Station, Tenn., December 14, 1863. Rutledge, Tenn., December 15, 1863. Dandridge, Tenn., December 25, 1863. Mossy Creek, Tenn., December 26, 1863. Kinsbro's X Roads, Tenn., January 16, 1864. Dandridge, Tenn., January 17, 1864. Fair Garden, Tenn., January 24, 1864. Sevierville, Tenn., January 27, 1864. Strawberry Plains, Tenn., January, 1864. Morristown, Tenn., March 19, 1864. Charles X Roads, Tenn., March 20, 1864. Cynthiana, Tenn., June 12, 1864. Siege of Atlanta, Ga., August 1 to September 3, 1864.

Stone Mountain, Ga., September 13, 1864. Lovejoy's Station, Ga., November 16, 1864. Clinton, Ga., November 19, 1864. Griswoldville, Ga., November 20, 1864. Macon, Ga., November 21, 1864. Milledgeville, Ga., November 24, 1864. Louisville, Ga., November 26, 1864. Waynesboro, Ga., November 28, 1864. Louisville, Ga., November 29, 1864. Waynesboro, Ga., December 4, 1864. Cypress Swamp, Ga., December 7, 1864. Near Savannah, Ga., December 9, 1864. Arnold's Plantation, Ga., December 11, 1864. Altamaha Bridge, Ga., December 17, 1864. Salkehatchie, S. C., February 6, 1865. White Pond, S. C., February 9, 1865. Aiken, S. C., February 11, 1865. Lexington, S. C., February 15, 1865. Broad River Bridge, S. C., February 17, 1865. Phillips' X Roads, N. C., March 4, 1865. Wadesboro, N. C., March 4, 1865. Solemn Grove, N. C., March 10, 1865. Averysboro, N, C., March 14 and 15, 1865. Bentonville, N. C., March 20 and 21, 1865. Raleigh & Smithfield R. R., N. C., April 11, 1865. Raleigh, N. C., April 12, 1865. Morrisville, N. C., April 13, 1865.

Tenth Cavalry.—House Mountain, Tenn., January, 1864. Bean's Gap, Tenn., March 26, 1864. Rheatown, Tenn., March 24, 1864. Jonesboro, Tenn., March 25, 1864. Johnsonville, Tenn., March 25, 1864. Watanga, Tenn., March 25, 1864. Powder Spring Gap, Tenn., April 28, 1864. Dandridge, Tenn., May 19, 1864. Greenville, Tenn., May 30, 1864. White Horn, Tenn., May 31, 1864. Morristown, Tenn., June 2, 1864. Bean's Station, Tenn., June 16, 1864. Rogersville, Tenn., June 17, 1864. Kingsport, Tenn., June 18, 1864. Cany Branch, Tenn., June 20, 1864. New Market, Tenn., June 21, 1864. Moseburg, Tenn., June 23, 1864. Williams Ford, Tenn., June 25, 1864. Dutch Bottom, Tenn., June 28, 1864. Sevierville, Tenn., July 5, 1864. Newport, Tenn., July 8, 1864. Morristown, Tenn., August 3, 1864. Greenville, Tenn., August 4, 1864. Mossy Creek, Tenn., August 18, 1864. Bull Gap, Tenn., August 21, 1864. Blue Spring, Tenn., August 23, 1864. Greenville, Tenn., August 23, 1864. Strawberry Plains, Tenn., August 24, 1864. Flat Creek Bridge, Tenn., August 24, 1864. Rogersville, Tenn., August 27, 1864. Bull Gap, Tenn., August 29, 1864. Greenville, Tenn., September 4, 1864. Sweet Water, Tenn., September 10, 1864. Thorn Hill, Tenn., September 10, 1864. Sevierville, Tenn., September 18, 1864. Jonesboro, Tenn., September 30, 1864. Johnson Station, Tenn., October 1, 1864. Watanga Bridge, Tenn., October 1 and 2, 1864. Chucky Bend, Tenn., October 10, 1864. Newport, Tenn., October 18, 1864. Irish Bottoms, Tenn., October 25, 1864. Madisonville, Tenn., October 30, 1864. Morristown, Tenn., November 20, 1864. Strawberry Plains, Tenn., November 23 and 24, 1864. Kingsport, Tenn., December 12, 1864. Bristol, Tenn., December 14, 1864. Saltville, Va., November 20, 1864. Chucky Bend, Tenn., January 10, 1865. Brabson's Mills, Tenn., March 25, 1865. Boonville, N. C., March 27, 1865. Henry Court House, Va., April 8, 1865. Abbott Creek, N. C., April 10, 1865. High Point, N. C., April 10, 1865. Statesville, N. C., April 14, 1865. Newton, N. C., April 17, 1865.

ELEVENTH CAVALRY.—Pound Gap, Ky., May 17, 1864. Hazel Green, Ky., May 10, 1864. Mount Sterling, Ky., June 9, 1864. Lexington, Ky., June 10, 1864. Georgetown, Ky., June 13, 1864. Cynthiana, Ky., June 12, 1864. Point Burnside, Ky., August 30, 1864. McCormack's Farm, Ky., September 23, 1864. Laurel Mountain, Va., September 29, 1864. Bowen's Farm, Va., September 30, and October 1, 1864. Saltville, Va., October 2, 1864. Sandy Mountain, Va., October 3 and 4, 1864. Western Virginia, October 5, 1864. Hazel Green, Ky., November 9, 1864. McCormack's Farm, Ky., November 10, 1864. Morristown, Ky., November 13, 1864. State Creek, Ky., November 14, 1864. Mount Sterling, Ky., November 16, 1864. Clinch River, Tenn., November 28, 1864. Russellville, Tenn., December 2, 1864. Morristown,

Tenn., December 2, 1864. Cobb's Ford, Tenn., December 3, 1864. Bristol, Tenn., December 13, 1864. Paperville, Tenn., December 13, 1864. Abington, Va., December 15, 1864. Wytheville, Va., December 16, 1864. Mount Airey, Va., December 17, 1864. Marion, Va., December 18, 1864. Seven Miles Ford, Va., December 19, 1864. Saltville, Va., December 20, 1864. Saltville, Va., December 21, 1864. Jonesboro, Va., December 23, 1864. Clinch River, Va., December 24, 1864. Morristown, Va., December 25, 1864. McCormack's Farm, Ky., December 29, 1864. Mount Sterling, Ky., January 19, 1865. Hazel Green, Ky., January 28, 1865. Flemingsburg, Ky., February 18, 1865. Boon, N. C., March 27, 1865. Yadkin River, N. C., March 28, 1865. Mount Airey, Va., March 31, 1865. Hillsville, Va., April 1, 1865. Salem, Va., April 3, 1865. Christiansburg, Va., April 3, 1865. Jonesboro, Tenn., April 5, 1865. Danbury, N. C., April 9, 1865. Statesville, N. C., April 10, 1865. Ford near Statesville, N. C., April 11, 1865. Salisburg, N. C., April 12, 1865. Statesville, N. C., April 13, 1865. Morganton, N. C., April 16, 1865. Morganton, N. C., April 17, 1865. Morganton, N. C., April 18, 1865. Swananoa Gap, N. C., April 19, 1865. Hendersonville, N. C., April 21, 1865. Ashville, N. C., April 25, 1865. Ward's Farm, N. C., April 28, 1865. Cæsar's Head, S. C., April 30, 1865. Pickensville, S. C., May 1, 1865. Anderson Court House, S. C., May 2, 1865.

Merrill Horse.—Memphis, Mo., July 18, 1862. Moor's Mill, Mo., July 28, 1862. Kirsville, Mo., August 6, 1862. Brownsville, Ark., August 25, 1863. Bayou Mecoe, Ark., August 27, 1863. Ashley's Bayou, Ark., September 7, 1863. Little Rock, Ark., September 10, 1863. Benton, Ark., September 11, 1863. Princeton, Ark., December 8, 1863. Little Mo. River, Ark., April 3 and 4, 1864. Prairie Dehan, Ark., April 12, 13, and 14, 1864. Camden, Ark., April 15, 1864. Jenkins' Ferry, Ark., April 29 and 30, 1864. Franklin, Mo.,

October 1, 1864. Otterville, Mo., October 10, 1864. Independence, Mo., October 22, 1864. Big Blue, Mo., October 23, 1864. Trenton Gap, Ga., March 22, 1865. Alpine, Ga., March 24, 1865. Summerville, Ga., March 25, 1865.

FIRST LIGHT ARTILLERY—BATTERY "A."—Rich Mountain, W. Va., July 11, 1861. Elkwater, W. Va., September 11, 12, 1861. Green Briar, W. Va., October 3, 1861. Bowling Green, Ky., February 14, 1862. Perryville, Ky., October 8, 1862. Bridgeport, Ala., April 29, 1862. Gunter's Landing, Ala., May 15, 1862. Athens, Ala., May 29, 1862. Whitesboro, Ala., June, 1862. Stone River, Tenn., December 31, 1862, January 1, 2, 3, 1863. Hoover's Gap, Tenn., June 25, 1863. Chickamauga, Tenn., September 19 and 20, 1863. Lookout Mountain, November, 1863. Mission Ridge, November 25, 1863.

BATTERY "B."—Pittsburg Landing, Tenn., April 6, 1862. Siege of Corinth, Miss., May 10 to 31, 1862. Corinth, Miss., October 3, 4, 1862. Resaca, Ga., May 9, 1864. Lay's Ferry, Ga., May 14, 1864. Calhoun Ferry, Ga., May 15, 1864. Rome X Roads, Ga., May 16, 1864. Cave Springs, Ga., October 13, 1864. Turkey Ridge, Ala., October 26, 1864. Griswold, Ga., November 22, 1864. Ogechee River, Ga., December 8, 1864. Savannah, Ga., December 11 to 20, 1864. Salkehatchie River, S. C., February 6, 1865. Columbia, S. C., February 15, 1865. Cox's Bridge, N. C., March 20, 1865. Bentonville, N. C., March 21, 22, 1865.

BATTERY "C."—Siege of Corinth, Miss., May 10 to 31, 1862. Farmington, Miss., May 9, 1862. Iuka, Miss., September 17, 19, 1862. Corinth, Miss., October 3, 4, 1862. Lumkin's Mills, Miss., November 29, 1862. Tallahatchie, Miss., November —, 1862. Town Creek, Ala., April, 1863. Resaca, Ga., May 14, 1864. Dallas, Ga., May 27, 1864. Big Shanty, Ga., June 15, 1864. Kenesaw, Ga., June 25, 1864. Nickajack Creek, Ga., July 1, 1864. Decatur, Ala., July 20,

1864. Siege of Atlanta, Ga., July 22 to August 25, 1864. Near Savannah, Ga., December 9, 10, 11, 1864. South Edisto, S. C., February 9, 1865. Cheraw, S. C., March 4, 1865. Fayetteville, N. C., March 13, 1865. Bentonville, N. C., March 21, 1865.

BATTERY "D."—Hoover's Gap, Tenn., June 26, 1863. Chickamauga, Tenn., September 19, 20, 1863. Chattanooga, Tenn., November 23, 24, 1863. Mission Ridge, Tenn., November 25, 1863. Nashville, Tenn., December 12 to 16, 1864.

BATTERY "E."—Pittsburg Landing, Tenn., April 7, 1862. Fort Riley, Tenn., September 20, 1862. Coosa, Ala., July 15, 1864. Cheraw, Ala., July 20, 1864. Nashville, Tenn., December 12 to 16, 1864.

BATTERY "F."—Richmond, Ky., 1862. Resaca, Ga., May 12, 1864. Lost Mountain, Ga., June 9, 11, 14, 1864. Moss House, Ga., June 22, 1864. Kenesaw, Ga., June 24, 1864. Marietta, Ga., July 1, 1864. Chattahoochie River, Ga., July 8, 1864. Decatur, Ga., July 18, 19, 1864. Atlanta, Ga., July 21, 1864. Utoy Creek, Ga., August 4, 1864. Siege of Atlanta, Ga., July 20 to August 25, 1864. Nashville, Tenn., December 12 to 16, 1864. Wise's Forks, N. C., March 10, 1865.

BATTERY "G."—Tazewell, Tenn., 1862. Cany Bottom, Ky., 1862. Chickasaw Bayou, Miss., December 28 and 29, 1862. Arkansas Post, Ark., January 6, 1863. Grand Gulf, Miss., April 28, 1863. Port Gibson, Miss., May 1, 1863. Champion Hills, Miss., May 16, 1863. Big Black River, Miss., May 17, 1863. Siege of Vicksburg, Miss., May 19 to July 4, 1863. Jackson, Miss., July 11 to 18, 1863. Fort Esperanza, Texas. November 29, 1863. Mobile, Ala., April 10, 1865.

BATTERY "H."—Thompson's Hills, Miss., May 1, 1863. Raymond, Miss., May 12, 1863. Jackson, Miss., May 14, 1863. Champion Hills, Miss., May 16, 1863. Vicksburg,

Miss., May 18, 1863. Siege of Vicksburg, Miss., May 19 to July 4, 1863. Brownsville, Miss., October, 1863. Clinton, Miss., February, 1864. Big Shanty, Ga., June 14, 1864. Kenesaw, Ga., June 27, 1864. Nickajack Creek, Ga., July 5, 1864. Peach Tree Creek, Ga., July 22, 1864. Siege of Atlanta, Ga., July 22, to August 25, 1864. Jonesboro, Ga., August 31, 1864. Lovejoy's Station, Ga., September 1, 1864.

BATTERY "I."—Aldie, Va., April 27, 1863. Gettysburg, Penn., July 3, 1863. Cassville, Ga., May 9, 1864. New Hope Church, Ga., May 27 and 28, 1864. Lost Mountain, Ga., June 17, 1864. Culp's House, Ga., July 1, 1864. Marietta, Ga., July 3, 1864. Peach Tree Creek, Ga., July 20, 1864. Siege of Atlanta, Ga., July 22 to August 25, 1864. Turner's Ferry, Ga., August 29, 1864.

BATTERY "K."—During the war the Battery was principally engaged on duty in fortifications, and on gunboats and transports, and saw much hard service. A portion of it assisted in repelling the attack of the rebel Gen. Wheeler's force on Dalton, Ga., in 1864.

BATTERY "L."—Triplett's Bridge, Ky., June 15, 1863. Lebanon, Ky., July 5, 1863. Buffington's Island, O., July 19, 1863. Steubenville, O., July 26, 1863. Salineville, O., July 26, 1863. Loudon, Tenn., September 2, 1863.

BATTERY "M."—Blue Springs, Tenn., October 10, 1863. Walker's Ford, Tenn., December 2, 1863. Tazewell, Tenn., January 21, 1864.

THIRTEENTH BATTERY.—The Battery was stationed in fortifications most of its service. On the 11th and 12th of July, 1864, it participated in the defense of Fort Stevens, near Washington, D. C., against the attack of the rebel General Early's forces, which then threatened the capital.

FOURTEENTH BATTERY.—During its term of service the Battery was principally on duty in fortifications, and took part in the defense of Washington, when it was attacked by the forces of General Early, in July, 1864, being engaged with the enemy on the 11th, 12th and 13th of that month.

First Sharp Shooters.—North Vernon, Ind., July 13, 1863. Pierceville, Ind., July 14, 1863. Wilderness, Va., May 5, 6 and 7, 1864. Ny River, Va., May 9, 1864. Po River, Va., May 10, 1864. Spottsylvania, Va., May 12, 13, 18, 1864. Oxford, Va., May 23, 1864. North Anna, Va., May 24, 25, 1864. Tolopotomy, Va., May 29, 1864. Bethesda Church, Va., June 2, 3, 1864. Coal Harbor, Va., June 7, 1864. Petersburg, Va., June 17, 18, 1864. The Crater, Va., July 30, 1864. Weldon R. R., Va., August 19, 21, 1864. Reams' Station, Va., August 25, 1864. Poplar Spring Church, Va., September 30, 1864. Pegram Farm, Va., October 2, 1864. Boydton Road, Va., October 8, 1864. Hatcher's Run, Va., October 27, 28, 1864. Fort Steadman, Va., March 25, 1865. Fort McGilvery, Va., April 1, 1865. Capture of Petersburg, Va., April 3, 1865. Siege of Petersburg, Va., from June 17, 1864, to April 3, 1865.

First Infantry (three months).—Bull Run, Va., July 21, 1861.

First Infantry (three years).—Mechanicsville, Va., June 26, 1862. Gaines' Mill, Va., June 27, 1862. Peach Orchard, Va., June 29, 1862. Savage Station, Va., June 29, 1862. Turkey Bend, Va., June 30, 1862. White Oak Swamp, Va., June 30, 1862. Malvern Hill, Va., July 1, 1862. Harrison's Landing, Va., July 2, 1862. Gainesville, Va., August 29, 1862. Bull Run, 2d, Va., August 30, 1862. Antietam, Md., September 17, 1862. Shepardstown Ford, Va., September 20, 1862. Snicker's Gap, Va., November 14, 1862. Fredericksburg, Va., December 13, 14, 1863. U. S. Ford, Va., January 1, 1863. Chancellorsville, Va., May 1, 2, 3, 4, 5, 1863. Kelly's Ford, Va., June 9, 1863. Ashby's Gap, Va., June 21, 1863. Gettysburg, Penn., July 2, 3, 4, 1863. Williamsport,

Md., July 12, 1863. Wapping Heights, Va., July 21, 1863. Culpepper, Va., October 13, 1863. Brandy Station, Va., October 13, 1863. Bristo Station, Va., October 14, 1863. Rappahannock Station, Va., November 7, 1863. Cross Roads, Va., November 26, 1863. Mine Run, Va., November 29, 1863. Wilderness, Va., May 5, 7, 1864. Laurel Hill, Va., May 8, 1864. Po River, Va., May 10, 1864. Spottsylvania, Va., May 12, 1864. Ny River, Va., May 21, 1864. North Anna, Va., May 23, 1864. Jerico Mills, Va., May 24, 1864. Noel's Turn, Va., May 26, 1864. Tolopotomy, Va., May 30, 1864. Magnolia Swamp, Va., June 1, 1864. Bethesda Church, Va., June 2, 1864. Petersburg, Va., June 18, 1864. Weldon R. R., Va., August 19, 20, 21, 1864. Peeble's Farm, Va., September 30, 1864. Hatcher's Run, Va., October 27, 1864. Nottaway Court House, Va., December 8, 1864. Dabney's Mills, or Hatcher's Run, February 6, 7, 1865. Hatcher's Run, Va., March 25, 1865. White Oak Road, Va., March 29, 1865. Five Forks, Va., April 1, 1865. Amelia Court House, Va., April 5, 1865. High Bridge, Va., April 6, 1865. Appomattox Court House, Va., April 9, 1865. Siege of Petersburg, Va., from June 17, 1864, to April 3, 1865.

SECOND INFANTRY.—Blackburn's Ford, Va., July 18, 1861. Bull Run, Va., July 21, 1861. Siege of Yorktown, Va., April 4 to May 4, 1862. Williamsburg, Va., May 5, 1862. Fair Oaks, Va., May 31 and June 1, 1862. Near Richmond, Va., June 18, 1862. Glendale, Va., June 30, 1862. Malvern Hill, Va., July 1, 1862. Bull Run, 2d, Va., August 28, 29, 30, 1862. Chantilly, Va., September 1, 1862. Fredericksburg, Va., December 12, 13, 14, 1862. Siege of Vicksburg, Miss., June 22 to July 4, 1863. Jackson, Miss., July 11 to 18, 1863. Blue Spring, Tenn., October 10, 1863. Loudon, Tenn., November 14, 1863. Lenoir Station, Tenn., November 15, 1863. Campbell's Station, Tenn., November 16, 1863. Siege of Knoxville, Tenn., November 17 to December 5, 1863. Knoxville, Tenn., November 24, 1863. Fort Saunders, Tenn., November 29, 1863. Thurley's Ford, Tenn., December 15, 1863. Strawberry Plains, Tenn., January 22, 1864. Near Knoxville, Tenn., January 24, 1864. Wilderness, Va., May 5, 6, 7, 1864. Ny River, Va., May 9, 1864. Spottsylvania, Va., May 10, 11, 12, 1864. Ox Ford, Va., May 23, 1864. North Anna, Va., May 24, 25, 1864. Tolopotomy, Va., May 30, 1864. Bethesda Church, Va., June 2 and 3, 1864. Coal Harbor, Va., June 7, 1864. Petersburg, Va., June 17, 18, 1864. The Crater, Va., July 30, 1864. Weldon R. R., Va., August 19, 21, 1864. Ream's Station, Va., August 25, 1864. Poplar Spring Church, Va., September 30, 1864. Pegram Farm, Va., October 2, 1864. Boydton Road, Va., October 8, 1864. Hatcher's Run, Va., October 27, 28, 1864. Fort Steadman, Va., March 25, 1865. Capture of Petersburg, Va., April 3, 1865. Siege of Petersburg, Va., from June 17, 1864, to April 3, 1865.

Third Infantry.—Blackburn's Ford, Va., July 18, 1861. Bull Run, Va., July 21, 1861. Siege of Yorktown, Va, April 4 to May 4, 1862. Williamsburg, Va., May 5, 1862. Fair Oaks, Va., May 31, 1862. Savage Station, Va., June 29, 1862. Peach Orchard, Va., June 29, 1862. Glendale, Va., June 30, 1862. White Oak Swamp, Va., June 30, 1862. Malvern Hill, Va., July 1, 1862. Bull Run, 2d, Va., August 29, 1862. Chantilly, Va., September 1, 1862. Fredericksburg, Va., December 13, 1862. Chancellorsville, Va., May 1, 2, 3, 1863. Gettysburg, Penn., July 2 and 3, 1863. Wapping Heights, Va., July 23, 1863. Auburn Heights, Va., October 1, 1863. Kelley's Ford, Va., November 7, 1863. Locust Grove, Va., November 27, 1863. Mine Run, Va., November 29, 1863. Wilderness, Va., May 5, 7, 1864. Todd's Tavern, Va., May 8, 1864. Po River, Va., May 10, 1864. Spottsylvania, Va., May 12, 1864. North Anna, Va., May 23, 24, 1864. Coal Harbor, Va., June 7, 1864. Petersburg, Va., June 16, 22, 1864. Deep Bottom, Va., July 27, 28, 1864. Strawberry Plains, Va., August 14, 17, 1864. Poplar Spring Church,

Va., September 30, 1864. Boydton Road, Va., October 27, 1864. Hatcher's Run, Va., February 2, March 25, 1864. Boydton Road, Va., April 2, 1864. Sailor's Creek, Va., April 6, 1864. New Store, Va., April 8, 1864. Appomattox Court House, Va., April 9, 1864. Siege of Petersburg, Va., from June 17, 1864, to April 3, 1865.

THIRD INFANTRY (re-organized).—Decatur, Ala., October 28, 29, 30, 1864. Murfreesboro, Tenn., Nov. 30 to December, 20, 1864.

FOURTH INFANTRY.—Bull Run, Va., July 21, 1861. New Bridge, Va., May 24, 1862. Hanover Court House, Va., May 27, 1862. Mechanicsville, Va., June 26, 1862. Gaines' Mills, Va., June 27, 1862. Savage Station, Va., June 29, 1862. Turkey Bend, Va., June 30, 1862. White Oak Swamp, Va., June 30, 1862. Malvern Hill, Va., July 1, 1862. Harrison's Landing, Va., July 2, 1862. Gainesville, Va., August 29, 1862. Bull Run, 2d, Va., August 30, 1862. Antietam, Md., September 17, 1862. Shepardstown Ford, Va., September 20, 1862. Snicker's Gap, Va., November 14, 1862. Fredericksburg, Va., December 13, 14, 1862. Morrisville, Va., December 30, 31, 1862. U. S. Ford, Va., January 1, 1863. Chancellorsville, Va., May 1, 2, 3, 4, 5, 1863. Kelly's Ford, Va., June 9, 1863. Ashby's Gap, Va., June 21, 1863. Gettysburg, Pa., July 2, 3, 4, 1863. Williamsport, Md., July 12, 1863. Wapping Heights, Va., July 21, 1863. Culpepper, Va., October 13, 1863. Brandy Station, Va., October 13, 1863. Bristo Station, Va., October 14, 1863. Rappahannock Station, Va., November 7, 1863. Cross Roads, Va., November 26, 1863. Mine Run, Va., November 29, 1863. Wilderness, Va., May 5, 6, 7, 1864. Laurel Hill, Va., May 8, 1864. Po River, Va., May 10, 1864. Spottsylvania, Va., May 12, 1864. Ny River, Va., May 21, 1864. North Anna, Va., May 23, 1864. Jerico Mills, Va., May 24, 1864. Noel's Turn, Va., May 26, 1864. Tolopotomy, Va., May 30, 1864. Magnolia Swamp,

Va., June 1, 1864. Bethesda Church, Va., June 2, 1864. Petersburg, Va., June 18, 1864. Weldon R. R., Va., August 19, 20, 21, 1864. Peebles' Farm, Va., September 30, 1864. Hatcher's Run, Va., October 27, 1864. Nottoway Court House, Va., December 8, 1864. Dabney's Mills, Va., February 6, 7, 1865. Hatcher's Run, Va., March 25, 1865. White Oak Road, Va., March 29, 1865. Five Forks, Va., April 1, 1865. Amelia Court House, Va., April 5, 1865. High Bridge, Va., April 6, 1865. Appomattox Court House, Va., April 9, 1865. Siege of Petersburg, Va., from June 17, 1864, to April 3d, 1865.

FOURTH INFANTRY (re-organized).—Decatur, Ala., October 28, 29, 30, 1864. New Market, Ala., November 19, 20, 1864. Murfreesboro, Tenn., November 30, to December 20, 1864.

FIFTH INFANTRY.—Pohick Church, Va., January 9, 1862. Siege of Yorktown, Va., April 4 to May 4, 1862. Williamsburg, Va., May 5, 1862. Fair Oaks, Va., May 31, 1862. Peach Orchard, Va., June 29, 1862. Glendale, Va., June 30, 1862. Malvern Hill, Va., July 1, 1862. Bull Run, 2d, Va., August 28, 1862. Grovetown, Va., August 29, 1862. Chantilly, Va., September 1, 1862. Fredericksburg, Va., December 13, 1862. The Cedars, Va., May 2, 1863. Chancellorsville, Va., May 3, 1863. Gettysburg, Penn., July 2 and 3, 1863. Wapping Heights, Va., July 23, 1863. Auburn Heights, Va., October 1, 1863. Kelly's Ford, Va., November 26, 1863. Locust Grove, Va., November 27, 1863. Mine Run, Va., November 29, 1863. Wilderness, Va., May 5 and 7, 1864. Todd's Tavern, Va., May 8, 1864. Po River, Va., May 10, 1864. Spottsylvania, Va., May 12, 1864. North Anna, Va., May 23, 1864. Tolopotomy, Va., May 30, 1864. Coal Harbor, Va., June 2, 1864. Petersburg, Va., June 16 and 22, 1864. Deep Bottom, Va., July 27 and 28, 1864. Strawberry Plains, August 14 and 17, 1864. Poplar Spring Church, Va.,

September 30, 1864. Boydton Road, Va., October 27, 1864. Hatcher's Run, Va., March 25, 1865. Boydton Road, Va., April 2, 1865. Capture of Petersburg, Va., April 3, 1865. Sailor's Creek, Va., April 6, 1865. New Store, Va., April 8, 1865. Appomattox Court House, Va., April 9, 1865. Siege of Petersburg, Va., from June 17, 1864, to April 3, 1865.

SIXTH INFANTRY.—Sewell's Point, Va., March 5, 1862. Port Jackson, La., April 25, 1862. Vicksburg, Miss., May 20, 1862. Grand Gulf, Miss., May 27, 1862. Amite River, Miss., June 20, 1862. Baton Rouge, La., August 5 and 17, 1862. Bayou Teche, La., January 14, 1863. Ponchetoola, La., March 24, 25, and 26, 1863. Barataria, La., April 7, 1863. Tickfaw River, La., April 12, 1863. Amite River, Miss., May 7, 1863. Ponchetoola, La., May 16, 1863. Siege of Port Hudson, May 23 to June 30, 1863. Tunica Bayou, La., November 8, 1863. Ashton, Ark., July 24, 1864. Fort Morgan, Ala., August 23, 1864. Spanish Fort, Ala., April, 1865. Fort Blakely, Ala., April, 1865. Fort Huger, Ala., April, 1865. Fort Tracey, Ala., April, 1865. Siege of Mobile, Ala., from March 20 to April 12, 1865.

SEVENTH INFANTRY.—Ball's Bluff, Va., October 21, 1861. Yorktown, Va., April 4 to May 4, 1862. West Point, Va., May 7, 1862. Fair Oaks, Va., May 31 to June 1, 1862. Peach Orchard, June 29, 1862. Savage Station, June 29, 1862. White Oak Swamp, Va., June 30, 1862. Glendale, Va., June 30, 1862. Malvern Hill, Va., July 1, 1862. Bull Run, 2d, Va., August 30, 1862. South Mountain, Md., September 14, 1862. Antietam, Md., September 17, 1862. Fredericksburg, Va., December 11, 12, and 13, 1862. Chancellorsville, Va., May 3 and 4, 1863. Haymarket, Va., June —, 1863. Gettysburg, Penn., July 2 and 3, 1863. Falling Waters, Md., July 14, 1863. Bristo Station, Va., November 27, 1863. Robinson's Tavern, Va., November 29, 1863. Mine Run, Va., November 29, 1863. Wilderness, Va., May 5 and

6, 1864. Po River, Va., May 10, 1864. Spottsylvania, Va., May 12, 1864. North Anna, Va., May 23, 1864. Ny River, Va., May 24, 1864. Tolopotomy, Va., May 30 and 31 and June 1, 1864. Coal Harbor, Va., June 3, 1864. Petersburg, Va., June 18 and 22, 1864. Deep Bottom, Va., July 27 and 28, 1864. Strawberry Plains, Va.,. August 14 and 17, 1864. Reams' Station, Va., August 25, 1864. Boydton Road, Va., October 27, 1864. Hatcher's Run, Va., February 5, 1865. Hatcher's Run, Va., March 29, 1865. Cat Tail Creek, Va., April 2, 1865. Farmville, Va., April 7, 1865. Siege of Petersburg, Va., from June 17, 1864, to April 3, 1865.

EIGHTH INFANTRY.—Port Royal, S. C., November 7, 1861. Coosaw River, S. C., December 18, 1861. Port Royal Ferry, S. C., January 1, 1862. Pocotaligo, S. C., April —, 1862. Fort Pulaski, Ga., April 14, 1862. Wilmington Island, Ga., April 16, 1862. James Island, S. C., June 16, 1862. Bull Run, 2d, Va., August 29, 1862. Chantilly, Va., September 1, 1862. South Mountain, Md., September 14, 1862. Antietam, Md., September 17, 1862. Fredericksburg, Va., Dec., 12, 13, and 14, 1862. Siege of Vicksburg, Miss., June 22 to July 4, 1863. Jackson, Miss., July 11 to 18, 1863. Blue Springs, Tenn., Oct. 10, 1863. Loudon, Tenn., November 14, 1863. Lenoir Station, Tenn., November 15, 1863. Campbell's Station, Tenn., November 16, 1863. Siege of Knoxville, Tenn., November 17 to December 5, 1863. Fort Saunders, Tenn., November 29, 1863. Wilderness, Va., May 5, 6, and 7, 1864. Spottsylvania, Va., May 10, 11, and 12, 1864. North Anna, Va., May 24 and 25, 1864. Bethesda Church, Va., June 2 and 3, 1864. Coal Harbor, Va., June 7, 1864. Petersburg, Va., June 17 and 18, 1864. The Crater, Va., July 30, 1864. Weldon R. R., Va., August 19 to 21, 1864. Reams' Station, Va., August 25, 1864. Poplar Spring Church, Va., September 30, 1864. Pegram Farm, Va., October 2, 1864. Boydton Road, Va., October 8, 1864. Hatcher's Run, Va., October

---

27 and 28, 1864. Fort Steadman, Va., March 25, 1865. Fort Mahon, Va,, April 2, 1865. Capture of Petersburg, Va., April 3, 1865. Siege of Petersburg, Va., from June 17, 1864, to April 3, 1865.

NINTH INFANTRY.—Murfreesboro, Tenn., July 13, 1861. Lavergne, Tenn., December 27, 1862. Stone River, Tenn., December 29 to 31, 1862, January 2 and 3, 1863. Chickamauga, Tenn., September 19 and 20, 1863. Mission Ridge, Tenn., November 25, 1863. Rocky Face, Ga., May 8, 1864. Resaca, Ga., May 14, 1864. Dallas, Ga., May 27, 1864. Kenesaw, Ga., June 25, 1864. Chattahoochie River, Ga., July 5 and 6, 1864. Siege of Atlanta, Ga., July 22 to August 25, 1864. Jonesboro, Ga., September 1, 1864.

TENTH INFANTRY.—Farmington, Miss., May 9, 1862. Siege of Corinth, Miss., May 10 to 31, 1862. Boonville, Miss., June 1, 1862. Nashville, Tenn., November 5, 1862. Stone River, Tenn., December 29 and 31, 1862, and January 2 and 3, 1863. Lavergne, Tenn., January 25, 1863. Antioch, Tenn., April 10, 1863. Mission Ridge, Ga., November 24, 1863. Chicamauga, Tenn., November 26, 1863. Ringold, Tenn., November 27, 1863. Buzzard's Roost, Ga., February 25, 1864. Resaca, Ga., May 15, 1864. Rome, Ga., May 18, 1864. Dallas, Ga., May 28, 1864. Kenesaw Mountain, Ga., June 27, 1864. Chattahoochie River, Ga., July 6, 1864. Peach Tree Creek, Ga., July 19, 1864. Durrant's Mill, Ga., July 20 and 21, 1864. Sandtown Road, Ga., August 14, 1864. Red Oak Turnout, Ga., August 27, 1864. Rough and Ready, Ga., August 30, 1864. Siege of Atlanta, Ga., July 22 to August 25, 1864. Atlanta, Ga., August 7, 1864. Jonesboro, Ga., September 1, 1864. Florence, Ala., October 6, 1864. Louisville, Ga., November 30, 1864. Savannah, Ga., December 11 to 21, 1864. Averysboro, N. C., March 16, 1865. Smithfield Roads, N. C., March 18, 1865. Bentonville, N. C., March 19 and 20, 1865.

ELEVENTH INFANTRY.—Gallatin, Tenn., August 13, 1862. Fort Riley, Tenn., September 1, 1862. Stone River, Tenn., December 29, 31, 1862, January 2, 3, 1863. Elk River, Tenn., July 1, 1863. Davis Cross Roads, Tenn., September 11, 1863. Chicamauga, Tenn., September 19, 20, 1863. Mission Ridge, Tenn., November 25, 1863. Graysville, Georgia, November 26, 1863. Buzzard's Roost, Ga., May 10, 1864. Resaca, Ga., May 14, 1864. New Hope Church, Ga., May 27, 1864. Kenesaw, Ga., June 22, 27, 1864. Rough Station, Ga., July 3, 4, 1864. Peach Tree Creek, Ga., July 20, 1864. Atlanta, Ga., August 7, 1864. Siege of Atlanta, Ga., July 22 to August 27, 1834.

ELEVENTH INFANTRY (re-organized).—This regiment was on duty in East Tennessee, guarding railroad, and on guard duty at Nashville during its term of service.

TWELFTH INFANTRY.—Pittsburg Landing, Tenn., April 6, 7, 1862, Iuka, Miss., September 19, 1862. Metamora, Tenn., October 5, 1862. Middleburg, Tenn., December 24, 1862. Mechanicsville, Miss., June 4, 1863. Siege of Vicksburg, Miss., June and July, 1863. Siege of Little Rock, Ark., August and September, 1863. Clarendon, Ark., June 26, 1864. Gregory's Landing, September 4, 1864.

THIRTEENTH INFANTRY.—Shiloh, Tenn., April 7, 1862. Farmington, Miss., May 9, 1862. Owl Creek, Miss., May 17, 1862. Corinth, Miss., May 27, 1862. Siege of Corinth, Miss., May 10 to 31, 1862. Stevenson, Ala., August 31, 1862. Mumfordsville, Ky., September 14, 1862. Perryville, Ky., October 8, 1862. Danville, Ky., October 17, 1862. Gallatin, Tenn., December 5, 1862. Mill Creek, Tenn., December 15, 1862. Lavergne, Tenn., December 27, 1862. Stewart's Creek, Tenn., December 29, 1862. Stone River, Tenn., December 29, 31, 1862, January 2, 3, 1863. Eagleville Tenn., January 20, 1863. Pelham, Tenn., July 2, 1863. Lookout Valley, Tenn., September 7, 1863. Lookout Mountain, Tenn., September 10,

---

1863. Chickamauga, Tenn., September 12, 18, 19, 1863. Chattanooga, Tenn., October 6, 1863. Mission Ridge, Tenn., November 26, 1863. Florence, Ala., October 8, 1864. Savannah, Ga., December 17, 18, 20, 21, 1864. Catawba River, S. C., February 29, 1865. Averysboro, N. C., March 16, 1865. Bentonville, N. C., March 19, 1865.

Fourteenth Infantry.—Farmington, Miss., May 9, 1862. Siege of Corinth, Miss., May 10 to 31, 1862. Lavergne, Tenn., November 1, 1862. Nashville, Tenn., November 5, 1862. Brentwood, Tenn., December 8, 1862. Stone River, Tenn., January 3, 1863. Weams' Springs, Tenn., July 27, 1863. Lawrenceburg, Tenn., November 4, 1863. Kenasaw, Ga., June 25, 1864. Chattahoochie River, Ga., July 5 and 6, 1864. Siege of Atlanta, Ga., July 22 to August 25, 1864. Atlanta, Ga., August 7, 1864. Jonesboro, Ga., September 1, 1864. Florence, Ala., October 10, 1864. Savannah, Ga., December 17 to 21, 1864. Fayetteville, N. C., March 12, 1865. Averysboro, N. C., March 16, 1865. Bentonville, N. C., March 19 and 20, 1855.

Fifteenth Infantry.—Pittsburg Landing, Tenn., April 6 and 7, 1862. Farmington, Miss., May 9, 1862. Siege of Corinth, Miss., May 10 to 31, 1862. Iuka, Miss., September 19, 1862. Chewala, Miss., October 1, 1862. Corinth, Miss., October 3 and 4, 1862. Siege of Vicksburg, Miss., June 11 to July 4, 1863. Jackson, Miss., July 11 to 18, 1863. Resaca, Ga., May 14, 1864. Big Shanty, Ga., June 15, 1864. Kenesaw, Ga., June 25, 1864. Decatur, Ga., July 20, 21, 1864. Siege of Atlanta, Ga., July 22 to August 25, 1864. Atlanta & M. R. R., Ga., August 29, 1864. Jonesboro, Ga., August 31, 1864. Lovejoy's Station, Ga., September 2, 1864. Clinton, Ga., November 20, 1864. Fort McAllister, Ga., December 13, 1864. Orangeburg, S. C., February 14 and 15, 1865. Congaree Creek, S. C., February 15, 1865. Saluda Creek, S. C., February 16, 1865. Columbia, S. C., February 17, 1865.

Fayetteville, N. C., March 13, 1865. Bentonville, N. C., March 19, 1865.

Sixteenth Infantry.—Siege of Yorktown, Va., April 4 to May 4, 1862. Hanover Court House, Va., May 27, 1862. Mechanicsville, Va., June 26, 1862. Gaines' Mills, Va., June 27, 1862. White Oak Swamp, Va., June 30, 1862. Turkey Bend, Va., June 30, 1862. Malvern Hill, Va., July 1, 1862. Harrison's Landing, Va., July 2, 1862. Ely's Ford, Va., August 29, 1862. Bull Run, 2d, Va., August 30, 1862. Antietam, Md., September 17, 1862. Shepardstown Ford, Va., September 19, 1862. Snicker's Gap, Va., November 4, 1862. U. S. Ford, Va., January 1, 1863. Chancellorsville, Va., April 30, May 2 to 5, 1863. Middleburg, Va., June 21, 1863. Gettysburg, Penn., July 1, 2, and 3, 1863. Williamsport, Md., July 12, 1863. Wapping Heights, Va., July 21, 22, 1863. Culpepper, Va., October 12 and 13, 1863. Brandy Station, Va., October 13, 1863. Bristo Station, Va., October 14, 1863. Rappahannock Station, Va., November 7, 1863. Cross Roads, Va., November 26, 1863. Mine Run, Va., November 26, 27, and 29, 1863. Wilderness, Va., May 5 to 7, 1864. Laurel Hill, Va., May 8, 1864. Po River, Va., May 10, 1864. Spottsylvania, Va., May 18, 1864. Ny River, Va., May 21, 1864. North Anna, Va., May 23, 1864. Noel's Turn, Va., May 26, 1864. Hanover, Va., May 29, 1864. Tolopotomy, Va., May 30, 1864. Magnolia Swamp, Va., June 1, 1864. Bethesda Church, Va., June 2, 3, and 4, 1864. Coal Harbor, Va., June 7, 1864. Gaines' Creek, Va., June 5, 1864. Petersburg, Va., June 18, 1864. Petersburg & Norfolk R. R., July 30, 1864. Weldon R. R., Va., August 19, 20, and 21, 1864. Peebles' Farm, Va., September 30, 1864. Hatcher's Run, Va., October 27, 1864. Dabney's Mills, or Hatcher's Run, Va., February 6 and 7, 1865. Hatcher's Run, Va., March 25, 1865. White Oak Road, Va., March 29, 1865. Quaker Road, Va., March 31, 1865. Five

Forks, Va., April 1, 1865. Amelia Court House, Va., April 5, 1865. High Bridge, Va., April 6, 1865. Appomattox Court House, Va., April 9, 1865. Siege of Petersburg, Va., from June 17, 1864, to April 3, 1865.

SEVENTEENTH INFANTRY.—South Mountain, Md., September 14, 1862. Antietam, Md., September 17, 1862. Fredericksburg, Va., December 12, 13, 14, 1862. Siege of Vicksburg, Miss., June 22 to July 4, 1863. Jackson, Miss., July 11 to 18, 1863. Blue Spring, Tenn., October 10, 1863. Loudon, Tenn., November 14, 1863. Lenoir Station, Tenn., November 15, 1863. Campbell's Station, Tenn., November 16, 1863. Siege of Knoxville, Tenn., November 17 to December 5, 1863. Thurley's Ford, Tenn., December 15, 1863. Fort Saunders, Tenn., December 29, 1863. Strawberry Plains, Tenn., January 22, 1864. Wilderness, Va., May 5, 6, and 7, 1864. Ny River, Va., May 9, 1864. Spottsylvania, Va., May 10, 11, 12, 1864. North Anna, Va., May 24, 1864. Bethesda Church, Va., June 2, 3, 1864. Coal Harbor, Va., June 7, 1864. Petersburg, Va., June 17, 18, 1864. The Crater, Va., July 30, 1864. Weldon R. R., Va., August 19, 21, 1864. Reams' Station, Va., August 25, 1864. Poplar Spring Church, Va., September 30, 1864. Pegram Farm, Va., October 2, 1864. Boydton Road, Va., October 8, 1864. Hatcher's Run, Va., October 27, 28, 1864. Fort Steadman, Va., March 25, 1865. Capture of Petersburg, Va., April 3, 1865. Siege of Petersburg, Va., from June 17, 1864, to April 3, 1865.

EIGHTEENTH INFANTRY.—Danville, Ky., February 24, 1863. Pond Springs, Ala., June 28, 1864. Curtiss Wells, Ala, June 24, 1864. Courtland, Ala., July 25, 1864. Athens, Ala., September 24, 1865. Decatur, Ala., October 24, November 28, 1865.

NINETEENTH INFANTRY.—Thompson's Station, Tenn., March 5, 1863. Nashville & Chattanooga R. R., Tenn., October 5, 1863. Resaca, Ga., May 15, 1864. Cassville, Ga., May

19, 1864. New Hope Church, Ga., May 25, 1864. Golgotha, Ga., June 15, 1864. Culp's Farm, Ga., June 22, 1864. Peach Tree Creek, Ga., July 20, 1864. Siege of Atlanta, Ga., July 22 to September 2, 1864. Savannah, Ga., December 11, 18, 20, 21, 1864. Averysboro, N. C., March 16, 1865. Bentonville, N. C., March 19, 1865.

Twentieth Infantry.—Fredericksburg, Va., December 12, 13, 14, 1862. Horse Shoe Bend, Ky., May 10, 1863. Siege of Vicksburg, Miss., June 22 to July 4, 1863. Jackson, Miss., July 11 to 18, 1863. Blue Springs, Tenn., October 10, 1863. Loudon, Tenn., November 14, 1863. Lenoir Station, Tenn., November 15, 1863. Campbell's Station, Tenn., November 16, 1863. Siege of Knoxville, Tenn., November 17 to December 5, 1863. Fort Saunders, Tenn., November 29, 1863. Thurley's Ford, Tenn., December 15, 1863. Strawberry Plains, Tenn., January 22, 1864. Chuckey Bend, Tenn., March 14, 1864. Wilderness, Va., May 5, 6, 7, 1864, Ny River, Va., May 9, 1864. Spottsylvania, Va., May 10, 11, 12, 1864. North Anna, Va., May 24, 25, 1864. Bethesda Church, Va., June 2 and 3, 1864. Coal Harbor, Va., June 7, 1864. Petersburg, Va., June 17, 18, 1864. The Crater, Va., July 30, 1864. Weldon R. R., Va., August 19, 21, 1864. Reams' Station, Va., August 25, 1864. Poplar Spring Church, Va., September 30, 1864. Pegram Farm, Va., October 2, 1864. Boydton Road, Va., October 8, 1864. Hatcher's Run, Va., October 27, 28, 1864. Fort Steadman, Va., March 25, 1865. Capture of Petersburg, Va., April 3, 1865. Siege of Petersburg, Va., from June 17, 1864, to April 3, 1865.

Twenty-First Infantry.—Perryville, Ky., October 8, 1862. Lavergue, Tenn., December 27, 1862. Stewart's Creek, Tenn., December 29, 1862. Stone River, Tenn., December 29, 31, 1862, and January 1, 2, and 3, 1863. Tullahoma, Tenn., June 24, 1863. Elk River, Tenn., July 1, 1863. Chickamauga, Tenn., September 19, 20, and 21, 1863. Chattanooga,

Tenn., October 6, 1863. Brown's Ferry, Tenn., October 27, 1863. Mission Ridge, Tenn., November 26, 1863. Savannah, Ga., December 11, 18, 20, and 21, 1864. Averysboro, N. C., March 16, 1865. Bentonville, N. C., March 19, 1865.

TWENTY-SECOND INFANTRY.—Danville, Ky., March 24, 1863. Hickman's Bridge, Ky., March 27, 1863. Pea Vine Creek, Tenn., September 17, 1863. McAffee's Church, Tenn., September 19, 1863. Chickamauga, Tenn., September 20, 1863. Wantahatchie, (near Chattanooga), Tenn., September 28 to October 28, 1863. Mission Ridge, Tenn., November 26, 1863. Atlanta, Ga., July 22 and 23, 1864.

TWENTY-THIRD INFANTRY.—Paris, Ky., July 29, 1863. Huff's Ferry, Tenn., November 12, 1863. Campbell's Station, Tenn., November 16, 1863. Siege of Knoxville, Tenn., November 17 to December 5, 1863. Dandridge, Tenn., January 14, 1864. Strawberry Plains, Tenn., January 22, 1864. Rocky Face, Ga., May 8, 1864. Resaca, Ga., May 14, 1864. Etowah River, Ga., May 22, 1864. Dallas, Ga., May 27, 1864. New Hope Church, Ga., June 1, 1864. Lost Mountain, Ga., June 17, 1864. Kenesaw, Ga., June 27, 1864. Chattahoochie River, Ga., July 5, and 6, 1864. Siege of Atlanta, Ga., July 22 to August 25, 1864. Lovejoy's Station, Ga., August 31, 1864. Columbia Tenn., November 25, 1864. Duck River, Tenn., November 28, 1864. Spring Hill, Tenn., November 29, 1864. Franklin, November 30, 1864. Nash-Tenn., December 12 to 16, 1864. Fort Anderson, N. C., February 18, 1865. Town Creek, N. C., February 20, 1865. Wilmington, N. C., February 21, 1865. Goldsboro, N. C., March 22, 1865.

TWENTY-FOURTH INFANTRY.—Fredericksburg, Va., December 12 and 13, 1862. Port Royal, Va., April 23, 1863. Fitzhugh Crossing, April 29, 1863. Chancellorsville, Va., May 3, 1863. Westmorland, Va., May 23, 1863. Gettysburg, Penn., July 1, 2, and 3, 1863. Mine Run, Va., November 29, 1863.

Raccoon Ford, Va., February, Va., February 5, 1864. Wilderness, Va., May 5, 6, and 7, 1864. Spottsylvania, Va., May 10, 11, and 12, 1864. North Anna, Va., May 28, 1864. Tolopotomy, Va., May 30, 1864. Coal Harbor, Va., June 1, 1864. Bethesda Church, Va., June 2, 3, and 4, 1864. Petersburg, Va., June 18, 1864. Weldon R. R., Va., August 18, 19, and 21, 1864. Hicksford, Va., December 9, 1864. Hatcher's Run, Va., October 27, 1864. Dabney's Mills, Va., February 6 and 7, 1865. Siege of Petersburg, Va., from June 17, 1864, to February 11, 1865.

TWENTY-FIFTH INFANTRY.—Mumfordsville, Ky., December 27, 1862. Tebb's Bend, Ky., July 4, 1863. Kingston, Tenn., November 26, 1863. Mossy Creek, Tenn,, December 29, 1863. Tunnel Hill, Ga., May 7 and 8, 1864. Rocky Face, Ga., May 9 and 10, 1864. Resaca, Ga., May 13 and 14, 1864. Cassville, Ga., May 19, 1864. Etowah River, Ga., May 20, 1864. Kingston, Ga., May 27, 1864. Altoona, Ga., May 26, 27, 28, and 29, 1864. Pine Mountain, Ga., June 3 to 7, 1864. Lost Mountain, Ga., June 10 to 18, 1864. Culp's Farm, Ga., June 22, 1864. Kenesaw, Ga., June 23 to 29, 1864. Nickajack Creek, Ga., July 1, 1864. Chattahoochie River, Ga., July 9, 1864. Decatur, Ga., July 18 and 19, 1864. Atlanta, Ga., July 20, 22, and 28, 1864. East Point, Ga., August 3, 1864. Utoy Creek, Ga., August 6, 1864. Siege of Atlanta, Ga., July 22 to August 25, 1864. Jonesboro, Ga., September 3 and 4, 1864. Rome, Ga., October 12, 1864. Cedar Bluffs, Ala., October 23, 1864. Pine Creek, Tenn., November 26, 1864. Franklin, Tenn., November 30, 1864. Nashville, Tenn,, December 15 and 16, 1864.

TWENTY-SIXTH INFANTRY.—Siege of Suffolk, Va., April 22 to May 14, 1863. Windsor, Va., May 22, 1863. Mine Run, Va., November 29, 1863. Wilderness, Va., May 5, 6, and 7, 1864. Corbin's Bridge, Va., May 8, 1864. Ny River, Va., May 9 and 10, 1864. Po River, Va., May 11, 1864.

Spottsylvania, Va., May 12, 13, 14, and 18, 1864. North Anna, Va., May 24, 1864. Tolopotomy, Va., May 30 and 31, and June 1, 1864. Coal Harbor, Va., June 2, 3, from 3 to 12 June, 1864. Petersburg, Va., June 16 and 17, 1864. Weldon R. R., Va., June 22, 1864. Deep Bottom, Va., July 27 and 28, 1864. Strawberry Plains, Va., August 14, 17, 1864. White Oak Swamp, Va., August 16, 1864. Reams' Station, Va., August 25, 1864. Peebles' Farm, Va., March 25, 1865. Hatcher's Run, Va., March 29, 1865. Boydton Road, Va., March 30, 31, 1865. White Oak Road, Va., March 31, 1865. Southerland's Station, Va., April 2, 1865. Amelia Springs, Va., April 5, 1865. Deatonsville, Va., April 6, 1865. Sailor's Creek, Va., April 6, 1865. High Bridge, Va., April 7, 1865. Farmville, Va., April 7, 1865. Appomattox Court House, Va., April 9, 1865. Siege of Petersburg, Va., from June 17, 1864, to April 3, 1865.

Twenty-Seventh Infantry.—Jamestown, Ky., June 2, 1863. Siege of Vicksburg, Miss., June 22 to July 4, 1863. Jackson, Miss., July 11 to 18, 1863. Blue Springs, Tenn., October 10, 1863. Loudon, Tenn., November 14, 1863. Lenoir Station, Tenn., November 15, 1863. Campbell's Station, Tenn., November 16, 1863. Siege of Knoxville, Tenn., November 17 to December 5, 1863. Fort Saunders, Tenn., November 29, 1863. Strawberry Plains, Tenn., January 22, 1864. Near Knoxville, Tenn., January 23, 1864. Wilderness, Va., May 5, 6, 7, 1864. Ny River, Va., May 9, 1864. Spottsylvania, Va., May 10, 11, 12, 1864. Oxford, Va., May 23, 1864. North Anna, Va., May 24, 25, 1864. Bethesda Church, Va., June 2 and 3, 1864. Coal Harbor, Va., June 7, 1864. Petersburg, Va., June 17, 18, 1864. The Crater, Va., July 30, 1864. Weldon R. R., Va., August 19, 21, 1864. Reams' Station, Va., August 25, 1864. Poplar Springs Church, Va., September 30, 1864. Pegram Farm, Va., October 2, 1864. Boydton Road, Va., October 8, 1864. Hatcher's Run, Va., October 27, 28, 1864. Fort Steadman, Va., March 25, 1865. Fort Mahon, Va., April 2, 1865. Capture of Petersburg, Va., April 3, 1865. Siege of Petersburg, Va., from June 17, 1864, to April 3, 1865.

TWENTY-EIGHTH INFANTRY.—Nashville, Tenn., December 12 to 16, 1864. Wise's Fork's, N. C., March 8, 9, 10, 1865.

TWENTY-NINTH INFANTRY.—Decatur, Ala., October 26, 27, 28, 1864. Overall Creek, Tenn., December 7, 1864. Winsted Church, Tenn., December 13, 1864. Shelbyville Pike, Tenn., December 15, 16, 1864. Nolansville, Tenn., December 17, 1864.

THIRTIETH INFANTRY.—This regiment was raised under authority from the War Department, for special service on the Michigan frontier, its term of service being for one year; and by orders from this Department, dated November 7, 1864.

FIRST MICHIGAN COLORED TROOPS (102d U. S.).—Baldwin, Fla., August 8, 1864. Honey Hill, S. C., November 30, 1864. Tullifinny, S. C., December 7, 1864. Devaux Neck, S. C., December 9, 1864. Cuckwold's Creek Bridge, February 8, 1865. Sampterville, S. C., April 8, 1865. Spring Hill, S. C., April 15, 1865. Swift Creek, S. C., April 17, 1865. Boykins, S. C., April 18, 1865. Singleton's Plantation, S. C., April 19, 1865.

We rose, and rushed unto her aid,
White faces sank into the grave,
Black faces, too, and all were brave.
Their red blood thrilled Columbia's heart;
It could not tell the two apart.

Aside from the acknowledged bravery and efficiency in battle, Michigan troops were, in a most remarkable manner, entrusted with posts of honor and great responsibility, which could scarcely have been accidental, but with a purpose.

The armies of no other nation, even after many years of the training which war brings with it, have evinced so marvelous a development of military capacity as characterized the American troops during their comparatively short term of service. The annals of the times will rear an imperishable monument to the patriotism of the States which, in the nation's peril, gave their sons in the conflict, and the honor of one will be among the precious possessions of the others; but it will be for Michigan to cherish with peculiar pride and tenderness the remembrance and the fame of the gallant band of patriots who, in the fiercest struggles of modern warfare, and among comrades of equal worth and bravery, while preserving the national life and integrity, have reflected undying lustre upon her own escutcheon.

And while we claim gallant services and noble deeds for Michigan troops, we must acknowledge and award bravery to their opponents. However much we may condemn their cause and repudiate their action, we must accord them a degree of courage and gallantry in battle worthy of Americans. For, although for the Federals in blue was reserved the laurel, they shared with the Confederates in grey the cypress, and while we claim the rose for the graves of our dead, we may afford to concede to theirs the lily.

> "From our dead foeman comes no chiding forth;
> We lie at peace; Heaven has no south or north;
> With roots of trees and flowers and fern and heather,
> God reaches down, and clasps our hands together."

The surrender of Lee and Johnson brought the rebellion to an end, almost as unexpected at the time by many, as its commencement was sudden and unlooked for.

The conquering armies of Grant and Sherman soon met in review at the National Capital: the greatest spectacle of the times. Proud days for the loyal North, but prouder still for the Union Armies; their fighting over, they had accomplished a result the greatest in history, the Union again united and rebound from its broken fragments as with bands of steel, all men made free within its borders, the shackles stricken from four million beings of God's creation, "*not for a day, but for all time.*"

Soon the Michigan regiments began to return. In cheers of welcome, the people greet them with gratitude and thanks. When the last reached the State, the lamented Crapo issued a well-timed proclamation, and says in the introductory paragraph:

"MICHIGAN SOLDIERS:—In the hour of National danger and peril, when the safety—when the very existence of your country was imperiled, you left your firesides, your homes, and your families to defend the Government and the Union. But the danger is now averted, the struggle is ended, and victory, absolute and complete victory, has perched upon your banners. You have conquered a glorious peace and are thereby permitted to return to your homes and the pursuit of tranquil industry, to which I now welcome you; and not only for myself, but for the people of the State, do I tender you a most cordial greeting."

A prophecy was generally advanced early in the war, and even up to its close, that idleness, debauchery and crime would characterize the release from military restraint, and the return to the State, of so many men who had been exposed to a service, judging from results in other armies, likely to engender irregular, improvident, and dissolute habits, leading to a lawless course of conduct, tending to the most deplorable consequences.

Alas for the prophets! their sayings were but the idle bablings of the most distrustful of humanity. By over ten years of experience since their return their theory has been completely refuted by a practice of honesty, virtue and thrift, most commendable, comparing favorably with our citizens generally, while many of them have filled the highest places in the administration of the State, and in the ordinary avocations in life.

The Michigan regiments were early in the field, and in rapid succession flung their flags to the breeze, until forty-nine regiments with several independent companies had gone to the front, to battle for the Union, and included up to the close of the war, over ninety thousand men, fourteen thousand and over of whom are recorded as martyrs for the country, on the parchment memorial, now in the capitol of the State, prepared under the direction of a grateful Legislature, approved by Governor Baldwin, and thus perpetuating their memories for future generations, to revere and honor.

While flags and banners are made the medium of expressing to troops gratitude for their patriotism, and the expectation of their gallant services, as well as their acknowledgment, costly monuments and columns are reared to commemorate their sacrifices.

From the earliest periods, in all civilized nations and communities, monuments have been acknowledged evidences of an enlighted, grateful, and generous people, and are so considered at the present day. Some are reared as mementoes of great national events, or as recognitions of achievements or acknowledged worth of individuals, others to honor the memories of patriots who have made sacrifice for their country; while the most numerous are raised to mark the last resting place of the departed, and to inscribe thereon their brief and latest history.

Some monuments, commenced with a national purpose, are in ruins ere completed. Others, undertaken by populous States or cities, are left unfinished, both speaking loudly of neglect, if not of disgrace, and at least are evidences of a cooled ardor in the cause, or of a wanton forgetfulness of the worth or valor which they were intended to perpetuate; while the humble stone with the tender and loving inscription of the widowed mother to her departed child is complete and stands intact, the consummation of a fixed and hallowed purpose.

A grateful recognition of the services of the defenders of the Republic in the recent war has been fully established in the hearts of the people, while a commendable disposition has been manifested to perpetuate their memories in the building of structures having that in view. In this respect the people of Michigan have performed their part in the erection of a costly State monument in honor of her "Martyrs who fell and the heroes who fought in defense of Union and Liberty."

The monument stands about forty-six feet, crowned by a colossal statute of Michigan ten feet high, a semi-civilized Indian Queen, with a sword in her right hand and a shield in her left; the figure in motion as if rushing forward in defense of her country. Beneath the plinth in which she stands are stars and wreaths. On the next section in front is the dedication, "Erected by the people of Michigan in honor of the martyrs who fell and the heroes who fought in defense of Liberty and Union." On the left are the arms of the State; on the right are the arms of the United States. On the projecting butments below are four allegorical figures seated. These figures, if standing, would be six and a half feet high, and they represent Victory, Union, Emancipation, and History. On the next section below, standing upon projecting butments are the defenders of Liberty and Union, the representations of the army and navy, four statues, seven feet high, soldiers of infantry, artillery, and cavalry, with a sailor of the navy. Between these statues, are bronze tablets, on which are medallion figures of Lincoln, Grant, Sherman, and Farragut. On the outer pedestals are four eagles.

The structure was designed by Randolph Rogers, the eminent American sculptor, a former citizen of Ann Arbor, Mich. It is of gray granite; the figures of superior bronze, were cast at Munich, Bavaria.

When the war had ended, the regiments returning, delivered to the State their Colors, not one dishonored, neither blot nor stain on their escutcheon, but all distinguished and glorious, bearing record of many battles, for they had been carried by the men who were with Wilcox and Richardson at Bull Run and Blackburn's Ford; men who stood with McClellan in West Virginia, on the Peninsula, and at South Mountain, and Antietam; with Grant at Shiloh; with Banks in the Shenandoah; with Burnside at Fredericksburg, at Knoxville, and at Jackson; with Butler in Louisiana; with Pope in Missouri and at Manassas; with Mulligan at Lexington, and with Sigel at Pea Ridge. Men who were with Hooker a Chancellorsville and in the battle above the clouds; with Mead at Gettysburg; with Grant at Vicksburg; with Rosecranz at Stone River and at Chickamauga; with Thomas at Mission Ridge; with Kilpatrick in his celebrated raid on Richmond; with Grant in the Wilderness, at Spottsylvania, Cold Harbor, and before Petersbuag; with Sheridan and Custar in the Shenandoah and at Five Forks; with Thomas at Nashville, and with Sherman in his great Atlanta campaign and on his unparalleled march to the sea. "The men who stood under the Flag of their countay, far away from home, in every quarter where the enemy was to be met;—along the banks of the father of wäters, in the great city at its mouths, on the Arkansas, in the captured forts of the Gulf, by the waters of the Cumberland, the Tennesseė, and of the Savannah, in the chief city of the south, among the conquering columns in the valley of the Shenandoah, and in the trenches, under the eye of the Lieutenant General in the great leagure of Petersburg and Richmond."

General Order No. 94, issued by the War Department, May 15th, 1865, directed that the volunteer regiments, returning to their respective States for final discharge, should deposit the regimental colors with the Chief Mustering Officer, to be held by him subject to the order of the Adjutant General of the army.

Under date of June 13th, 1865, the War Department authorized the Chief Mustering Officer of this State, to turn over to the Governor, at his request, all the regimental colors of Michigan regiments, then in his charge, or that might thereafter come into his possession, under the provisions of the order referred to.

Extract from the letter of Major John H. Knight, U. S. Army, accompanying the delivery of the flags:

"OFFICE CHIEF MUSTERING OFFICER,
Detroit, Mich., June 19th, 1866.

"*Brigadier General John Robertson, Adjutant General State of Michigan, Detroit, Mich.:*

"GENERAL—All the regiments sent from the State of Michigan, to put down the rebellion of the Southern States, having now been mustered out of service, paid off and disbanded, the time has arrived when I should, in compliance with orders from the War Department, deliver to the Governor of the State, the flags turned over to me by the officers of the disbanded regiments.

"I have the honor, this day, to deliver to you (you being at the head of the State Military Bureau and its chief officer), all of them in my possession.

"Please find a list of the flags inclosed. In turning them over to you I am sensibly reminded that they are the flags under which so many brave and successful deeds have been performed—so many valuable lives given up in the cause of the Union and republican liberty, and such beneficial results obtained.

* * * * * * *

"By depositing these flags with the State authorities, in each State, the authorities of the Government have placed therein a monument in memory of its glories which will be most cherished, and whenever beheld by the people will far surpass, in the feelings of veneration which they will call forth, all the pillars of marble or granite which human genius could build. It will be remembered that they have passed through the scenes of strife, and that they have been carried by the hands of the brave men themselves, who fought and died for our national liberties; it will be seen that on them is inscribed the names of the battles passed through, where the fate of liberty was staked and decided; and with what feelings of reverence will these strips of bunting be looked upon by the father, mother, brother or sister, whose son or brother marched to victory or glorious death under their folds. Whilst all patriots on viewing these Battle Flags will remember and mourn the loss of life and regret the vast expenditures which have been made to preserve our liberties, yet all will rejoice over the glorious results which have been achieved.

"Permit me to congratulate, through you, the people of Michigan, for the brilliant and conspicuous part performed by Michigan regiments in the late war for the Union. I believe there is no blot upon their record, but all is bright, conspicuous and glorious, whilst an extraordinary number of personal distinctions shine upon the pages."

Next of interest to the men who upheld and defended them in the field, are the colors themselves. They are, aside from that, indelibly stamped on the hearts of the people, the most forcible mementoes of the gallant Regiments that so heroically stood by them and the country, even in the darkest days of the war.

They were as little specs in the long lines of the great American Armies, yet they were often watched in the advancing columns, with intense anxiety, but with strong confidence and hope by the greatest Generals of the land.

To bear them aloft was a signal for rebel bullets, often bringing swift and certain death, but they were never trailed in the dust, nor lacked a gallant bearer.

On the Fourth of July, 1866, those colors were formally presented in Detroit, through the Governor to the State, and were deposited in its archives to be sacredly kept and carefully pre served.

The setting apart of the National birthday for the purpose was most appropriate. Its hallowed memories reminded the people of the gallant struggle of their forefathers in establishing the Government, in the maintenance of which so many present had followed their Flags to glorious victory.

A cordial invitation had been extended by the Governor to all who had served in the war, and for the purpose of honoring the day, and especially the occasion, as well as giving the people of the State an opportunity to witness the emblems of State prowess, and of patriotism, bravery, and gallant services, a procession was arranged and carried into effect.

The procession was under the direction of General James E. Pittman, who at the time was Inspector General of the State, and who was selected and appointed by the Governor as Chief Marshal of the day.

For the presentation of the Colors in behalf of the regiments, Major General O. B. Willcox was in like manner chosen, being the first Colonel who left the State for the field with a Michigan regiment.

The returned troops were commanded by Brevet Brigadier General William L. Stoughton, the ranking Colonel then in the State, amongst those who belonged to their regiments at the time of the muster out of their respective organizations.

The divisions were organized as follows, and the regiments took position in them in the following order:

FIRST DIVISION—BREVET MAJ. GEN. R. H. G. MINTY, COMMANDING.

1st Regiment Engineers and Mechanics.

1st, 2d, 3d, 4th, 5th, 6th, 7th, 8th, 9th, 10th, and 11th Regiments Cavalry.

Companies H, I, and L, Merrill Horse.

1st Regiment Light Artillery—Batteries A, B, C, D, E, F, G, H, I, K, L, and M, and 13th and 14th Batteries Light Artillery.

1st Regiment Sharp-shooters.

Companies C, I, and K, 1st U. S. Sharp-shooters.

Company B, 2d U. S. Sharp-shooters.

Michigan Companies that served as such in Regiments of other States.

Soldiers belonging to this State who served in Regiments of other States, not in Michigan Companies.

Michigan soldiers and sailors who served in the regular army and navy.

SECOND DIVISION—BREVET MAJ. GEN. H. A. MORROW, COMMANDING.

1st (3 months), 1st (3 years), 2d, 3d, 3d (reorganized), 4th, 4th (reorganized), 5th, 6th (Heavy artillery), 7th, 8th, 9th, 10th Regiments Infantry.

THIRD DIVISION—BREVET BRIG. GEN. O. L. SPAULDING, COMMANDING.

11th, 11th (reorganized), 12th, 13th, 14th, 15th, 16th, 17th, 18th, 19th, 20th Regiments Infantry.

FOURTH DIVISION—BREVET BRIG. GEN. HEBER LE FAVOUR, COMMANDING.

21st, 22d, 23d, 24th, 25th, 26th, 27th, 28th, 29th, 30th Regiments Infantry; 1st Regiment (102 U. S.) Michigan Colored Troops.

"I saw the soldiers come to-day
From battle-fields afar;
No conqueror rode before their way,
On his triumphal car;
But Captains, like themselves, on foot,
And banners sadly torn,
All grandly eloquent, though mute,
In pride and glory borne."

These divisions, composed of the Veterans of the respective regiments, carrying their old Colors, presented the finest appearance possible. It was remarkable with what pride each

Color-bearer held aloft the banner under which he had served, and with what elasticity of step and erect bearing the whole marched to the strains of the martial music, to which they had been so long accustomed.

The State authorities were cheerfully aided and liberally sustained by the citizens of Detroit, and the affair was honored by a magnificent celebration, and participated in by the most numerous assembly of people from all parts of the State ever congregated within its borders.

The invitation extended by the Governor to the soldiers, was well responded to, and they rallied in great numbers under their old banners as in times past, presenting them to the State, as follows:

First Infantry (3 months), one; First Infantry (3 years), seven; Second Infantry, two; Third Infantry (re-organized), two; Fourth Infantry (re-organized), one; Fifth Infantry, five; Sixth Heavy Artillery, two; Seventh Infantry, one; Eighth Infantry, four; Ninth Infantry, three; Tenth Infantry, two; Eleventh Infantry, one; Eleventh Infantry (re-organized), two; Twelfth Infantry, four; Thirteenth Infantry, four; Fourteenth Infantry, four; Fifteenth Infantry, four; Sixteenth Infantry, four; Seventeenth Infantry, four; Eighteenth Infantry, two; Nineteenth Infantry, one; Twentieth Infantry, two; Twenty-first Infantry, four; Twenty-second Infantry, two; Twenty-third Infantry, two; Twenty-fourth Infantry, seven; Twenty-fifth Infantry, two; Twenty-sixth Infantry, five; Twenty-seventh Infantry, five; Twenty-eighth Infantry, two; Twenty-ninth Infantry, two; Thirtieth Infantry, two; First Engineers and Mechanics, four; First Sharp-Shooters, one; First Cavalry, two; Third Cavalry, one; Fourth Cavalry, one; Fifth Cavalry, one; Sixth Cavalry, one; Seventh Cavalry, three; Eighth Cavalry, one; Ninth Cavalry, one; Tenth Cavalry, one; Eleventh Cavalry, one; Battery "B," one; Battery "E," one; Battery "F," one; Battery "H," two; Battery "I," one; Battery "K," two; Fourteenth Battery, one; First Colored Infantry (102d U. S.), three.

These Flags bear the National and State emblems, and are the cherished and venerated mementos of great public services rendered by the soldiers of the State to the Republic, and of Regimental bravery.

Around them will cluster hallowed memories of State pride, of National grandeur and prowess, of individual heroism and patriotism, of fallen comrades and family bereavements.

"Those banners soiled with dust and smoke,
And rent by shot and shell,
That through the serried phalanx broke,
What terrors could they tell!
What tales of sudden pain and death—
In every cannon's boom—
When e'en the bravest held his breath,
And waited for his doom."

At the close of the procession, which was one of the finest and most interesting displays ever witnessed in Michigan, the veterans were massed in front of the speaker's stand on Campus Martius, and delivered their Flags to the Governor, when, after a prayer by Bishop S. A. McCoskry, appropriate addresses were made, from which the following extracts are taken:

WELCOMING ADDRESS OF MAYOR M. I. MILLS.

* * * * * * *

You have permitted no rebel hand to tear them from your grasp, and bear them trophies to the foes of our Union. But, with Spartan fidelity, true to the trust confided, you have returned them home again, now to be placed in the archives of the State, there to remain mournful relics and mementoes of our cruel and bloody strife, a warning to all; and we have yet to learn that our State, or a single Michigan Flag, has ever been dishonored upon a battle-field. You have now forsaken the tented field for the peaceful pursuits of citizen life. You now rest from your dangers and your toils. You have the proud consciousness of knowing that you are among the defenders and preservers of our Union. You have the satisfaction of again seeing the old Flag, the Flag of our fathers, wave defiantly and triumphantly over every foot of our national domain. Your prowess and your victories have rejoiced every patriot heart in the land. A nation's gratitude is yours. The orphans of your brave comrades are entitled to your paternal care. They must be ranked as children of the State. Amid our happiness and our rejoicings upon this glorious anniversary of our country, we cannot forget that our countrymen—our erring and misguided countrymen of the South, are still smarting under the blows that justice and patriotism compelled you to inflict. Shall we not show to the penitent that we are as magnanimous in peace as we have been irresistible in war? Shall we not imitate the examples of your most illustrious generals, Grant and Sherman, that brave men do not trample upon a fallen foe? Shall we ignore the meek and lowly teachings of Him who died upon the cross? God forbid!

* * * * * * *

PRESENTATION ADDRESS OF GENERAL O. B. WILLCOX.

* * * * * * *

"Of all these Flags there is scarcely one which has not waved in the thickest of the fight; scarcely a color which has not seen its heroic bearers one after another struck down in battle. Ah! yes, many a hand that vigorously grasped these Flag-staffs and led the van, now lies crumbling in the grave; and not color-bearers alone, but nearly 15,000 others who fought beside them—the flower of Michigan—return not to receive your thanks and the plaudits of their grateful countrymen. They walk the earth no more in the flesh, but their fame survives, and their glorified forms bend above us, now, and with hands unseen deck these colors with invisible garlands. While we have souls to remember, let their memories be cherished. Let a monument be erected to them—at once worthy of their deeds and worthy of the State; let their widows and orphans be cared for; and never let us forget the cause for which they fell; a war not for ambition, not for a dynasty or a party—no, let party spirit be hushed in their majestic presence—not to establish or defend a throne, neither for spoils, oppression, nor any other unworthy object, but simply for the Union, and as soon as may be let the ancient foundations of the Constitution be restored with only the crumbling stone of slavery left out, and with liberty guaranteed to all.

"I have seen the finger of Providence through the thick smoke of battle, and now that the dark curtain is lifted, and the sun of victory breaks through in meridian splendor, I have more confidence than ever in our destiny. We thank God that we have returned to our homes victorious. If you, the Governor and people of Michigan, are satisfied with the manner in which we have performed our part, we are grateful for your applause. We have tried to do our duty, and we have done no more than that duty which every citizen owes to a free and fraternal government, and in the peaceful walks of civil life we shall endeavor to set an example of peace, moderation, and submission to the laws. It only now remains for me, in the name of the Michigan soldiers, to surrender to the State these Flags, tattered but not stained, emblems of a war that is past. We shall ever retain our pride in their glorious associations, as well as our love for the old Peninsular State."

* * * * * * *

RECEPTION SPEECH OF GOVERNOR HENRY H. CRAPO.

* * * * * * *

"I receive, in behalf of the people of Michigan, these honorable memorials of your valor and the nation's glory; and on their part, I once more thank you for the noble services you have rendered in defending and preserving the life of the nation, at the hazard of your own, and at the sacrifice of so many of your comrades. I may venture to give you the assurance that you have the unbounded gratitude and love of your fellow-citizens; and that between you and them the glory of these defaced old Flags will ever be a subject of inspiration—a common bond of affection. To you they represent a nationality which you have periled your lives to maintain; and are emblematic of a liberty which your strong arms and stout hearts have helped to win. To us they are our fathers' Flags—the ensigns of all the worthy dead—your comrades, our relatives and friends—who for their preservation have given their blood to enrich the battle-fields, and their agonies to hallow the prison-pens of a demoniac enemy. They are your Flags and ours. How rich the treasure! They will not be forgotton and their history left unwritten.

Their stories will be as household words; and the minds of those who come after us will dwell upon the thoughts of manly endeavor, of staunch endurance, of illustrious achievement, which their silent eloquence will ever suggest. They will ever typify the grand results accomplished by the loyal men of the nation in this great rebellion: and should the flame of patriotism ever wane upon our altar-stone, the halo from these mementos will kindle again the ancient fire that electrified the world.

Let us, then, tenderly deposit them, as sacred relics, in the archives of our State, there to stand forever, her proudest possession—a revered incentive to liberty and patriotism, and a constant rebuke and terror to oppression and treason."

* * * * * * *

The ceremony concluded with a benediction by the Rev. Dr. George Duffield, when the veterans marched to the depot of the Michigan Central Railroad, where they partook of a substantial repast, prepared for them by the citizens.

Those old Flags, fluttering proudly in the breeze, bearing the mark of many bullets, and the record of many battles, under which friends had fought, and loved ones fallen, strengthened the people in their love of country, and made them firmer in their faith of the lasting union of the republic. They were gladdened in heart at the presence of the veterans of the army of Michigan. Yet, alas! their joy was mixed with sorrow, fourteen thousand and over of that army had joined the "Legion of the dead," they had fallen under the Flag, on many battle-fields. Most of them, in a spirit of humanity and veneration, have been gathered by kindly hands into the beautiful cemeteries, provided by a beneficent government, and now sleep in their windowless palaces of rest, where they will lie in peace until the last reveille; but some of them yet lie where their comrades left them, by the way-sides, on the sunny brows of many hills, in the dense forests, in the valleys, and under the orange and palm trees, on the banks of rivers, under the deep, dark waters, and on the sea beach, where the restless waves forever chant their requiem. But they lie under the Flag they defended, and made stainless, and in the land they saved and made free.

"Thank God! there beams o'er land and sea,
Our blazing star of victory;
And every where from main to main,
The 'Old Flag' flies and rules again."

APPENDIX.

APPENDIX.

Places and dates at which Michigan troops encountered the enemy during the war, carefully compiled from the official reports of Regimental Commanders, and covering over eight hundred occasions where Michigan men defended and protected the Flag against treason and armed rebellion.

Abbott Creek, North Carolina, April 10, 1865.
Abington, Virginia, December 13, 1864.
Ackworth, Tennessee, June 2 to 5, 1864.
Aiken, South Carolina, February, 11, 1865.
Aldie, Virginia, April 27, 1863.
Altamaha Bridge, Georgia, December 17, 1864.
Altoona, Georgia, May 26 to 29, 1864.
Amelia Court House, Virginia, April 5, 1865.
Amite River, Mississippi, June 20, 1862.
Amite River, Mississippi, May 7, 1863.
Alpine, Georgia, March 23, 1865.
Alexandria, Tennessee, April 23, 1863.
Anderson's Cross Roads, Tennessee, October —, 1863.
Anderson's Court House, South Carolina, May 2, 1865.
Antietam, Maryland, September 17, 1862.
Antioc, Tennessee, April 10, 1863.
Appomattox Court House, Virginia, April 8 and 9, 1865.
Arkansas Post, Arkansas, January 6, 1863.
Arnolds' Plantation, Georgia, December 11, 1864.
Arundell Creek, Georgia, May 16, 1864.
Ashby's Gap, Virginia, June 21, 1863.
Ashley's Bayou, Arkansas, September 7, 1863.
Ashton, Arkansas, July 24, 1864.

Ashville, North Carolina, April 25, 1865.
Athens, Tennessee, September 27, 1863.
Athens, Alabama, May 29, 1862.
Athens, Alabama, September 24, 1865.
Atlanta, Georgia, siege of, July 22 to August 25, 1864.
Auburn, Tennessee, February 19, 1863.
Auburn Heights, Virginia, October 1, 1863.
Averysboro, North Carolina, March 14 and 15, 1865.
Bacon Creek, Kentucky, December 24, 1862.
Baird's Mill, Tennessee, November 30, 1862.
Baldwin, Mississippi, June —, 1862.
Ball's Bluff, Virginia, October 21, 1861.
Baldwin, Florida, August 8, 1864.
Barataria, Louisiana, April 7, 1863.
Baton Rouge, Louisiana, August 5, 1862.
Baton Rouge, Louisiana, August 17, 1862.
Baltimore Cross Roads, Virginia, May 29, 1864.
Bay Springs, Mississippi, September 10, 1862.
Bayou Teche, Louisiana, January 14, 1863.
Bayou Mecoe, Arkansas, August 27, 1863.
Beaver Dam Station, Virginia, May 10, 1864.
Bean's Station, Tennessee, December 14, 1863.
Bean's Station, Tennessee, June 16, 1864.
Bean's Gap, Tennessee, March 26, 1864.
Bentonville, North Carolina, March 20 and 21, 1865.
Bentonville, North Carolina, March 19, 1865.
Benton, Arkansas, September 11, 1863.
Berryville, Virginia, September 3, 1864.
Berryville, Kentucky, October 8, 1862.
Bethesda Church, Tennessee, November 29, 1864.
Bethesda Church, Virginia, June 2 and 3, 1864.
Big Shanty, Georgia, June 9, 1864.
Big Shanty, Georgia, June 15, 1864.
Big Black River, Mississippi, May 17, 1863.
Big Blue, Missouri, October 23, 1864.

Blackland, Mississippi, June 5, 1862.
Blackburn Ford, Virginia, July 18, 1861.
Blountsville, Tennessee, —— —, 1862.
Blue Springs, Tennessee, August 23, 1864.
Blue Springs, Tennessee, October 5 to 10, 1863.
Boonsboro, Maryland, July 6, 1863.
Boonsboro, Maryland, July 8, 1863.
Boonville, Mississippi, June 1, 1862.
Boonville, North Carolina, March 27, 1865.
Boon, North Carolina, March 27, 1864.
Bower's Farm, Virginia, September 30 and October 1, 1864.
Bowling Green, Kentucky, February 14, 1862.
Boydton Road, Virginia, October 8, 1864.
Boydton Road, Virginia, October 27, 1864.
Boydton Road, Virginia, April 2, 1864.
Boykins, South Carolina, April 18, 1865.
Brandy Station, Virginia, October 13, 1863.
Bradyville, Tennessee, January 21, 1863.
Brabson's Mills, Tennessee, March 25, 1865.
Brentwood, Tennessee, December 8, 1862.
Bridgeville, Alabama, April 6, 1865.
Bristol, Tennessee, December 14, 1864.
Bristol, Tennessee, December 13, 1864.
Bridgeport, Alabama, April 29, 1862.
Bristo Station, Virginia, October 14, 1863.
Brontwood, Tennessee, March 25, 1863.
Brownsville, Mississippi, January 14, 1863.
Brownsville, Mississippi, October —, 1863.
Broad River Bridge, South Carolina, February 17, 1865.
Brown's Ferry, Tennessee, October 27, 1863.
Brownsville, Arkansas, August 25, 1863.
Buckland's Mills, Virginia, October 19, 1863.
Buffington's Island, Ohio, July 19, 1863.
Bull Run, Virginia, July 21, 1861.

Bull Run 2d, Virginia, August 28, 29, and 30, 1862.
Bull Gap, Tennessee, August 21, 1864.
Bull Gap, Tennessee, August 29, 1864.
Buzzard's Roost, Georgia, February 25, 1864.
Buzzard's Roost, Georgia, May 10, 1864.
Byhalia, Mississippi, October 12, 1863.
Cæsar's Head, South Carolina, April 30, 1865.
Calhoun, Tennessee, September 26, 1863.
Calhoun Ferry, Georgia, May 15, 1864.
Campbellville, Tennessee, September 5, 1864.
Campbellville, Tennessee, November 24, 1864.
Campbell Station, Tennessee, November 16, 1863.
Camden, Arkansas, April 15, 1864.
Cany Branch, Tennessee, June 20, 1864.
Capture of Jeff. Davis, Georgia, May 10, 1865.
Carter's Station, Tennessee, September 21, 1863.
Cassville, Georgia, May 9, 1864.
Cassville, Georgia, May 19, 1864.
Cat Tail Creek, Virginia, April 2, 1865.
Catawba River, South Carolina, February 29, 1865.
Cavetown, Maryland, July 5, 1863.
Cave Springs, Georgia, October 13, 1864.
Cedar Mountain, Virginia, August 9, 1862.
Cedar Creek, Virginia, August 19, 1864.
Cedar Bluffs, Alabama, October 23, 1864.
Chattanooga, Tennessee, October 6, 1863.
Chattanooga, Tennessee, November 17, 1863.
Chattanooga, Tennessee, November 23 and 24, 1863.
Charlotte, Tennessee, February 6, 1863.
Chattahoochie, Georgia, July 4, 1864.
Chattahoochie, Georgia, July 5 and 6, 1864.
Chattahoochie, Georgia, July 8, 1864.
Chattahoochie, Georgia, July 9, 1864.
Charles' Cross Roads, Tennessee, March 20, 1864.

Champions Hills, Mississippi, May 16, 1863.
Chancellorsville, Virginia, May 1 to 6, 1863.
Chantilly, Virginia, September 1, 1862.
Cherry Valley, Tennessee, June 16, 1863.
Cheraw, South Carolina, March 4, 1865.
Chewala, Mississippi, October 1, 1862.
Chickamauga, Tennessee, September 18, 19, 20, 1863.
Chickamauga, Tennessee, November 26, 1863.
Chickasaw Bayou, Mississippi, December 28, 29, 1862.
Christianburg, Virginia, April 3, 1864.
Chucky Bend, Tennessee, October 10, 1864.
Chucky Bend, Tennessee, January 10, 1865.
Clarendon, Arkansas, June 26, 1864.
Cleveland, Tennessee, December 12, 1863.
Cleveland, Tennessee, September 18, 1863.
Clifton, Mississippi, February 10, 1863.
Clinton, Georgia, November 19, 1864.
Clinch River, Virginia, November 28, 1864.
Clinch River, Virginia, December 24, 1864.
Clinton, Mississippi, February —, 1864.
Coal Harbor, Virginia, May 30, and June 1, 1864.
Coal Harbor, Virginia, June 2 to 12, 1864.
Coal Harbor, Virginia, July 21, 1864.
Cobb's Ford, Tennessee, December 3, 1864.
Coffeeville, Mississippi, December 5, 1862.
Columbia, Tennessee, March 4 and 5, 1863.
Columbia, Tennessee, November 25, 26, 27, 1863.
Columbia, South Carolina, February 15, 1865.
Columbia, South Carolina, February 17, 1865.
Congaree Creek, South Carolina, February 15, 1865.
Coosa, Alabama, July 15, 1864.
Coosaw River, South Carolina, December 18, 1861.
Corinth, Mississippi, Siege of, May 10 to 31, 1862.
Corinth, Mississippi, October 3 and 4, 1862.
Corinth, Mississippi, February —, 1865.

Corbin's Ridge, Virginia, May 8, 1864.
Cotton Port, Tennessee, September 30, 1863.
Courtland, Alabama, July 25, 1864.
Covington, Georgia, July 22, 1864.
Covington, Georgia, July 28, 1864.
Cox's Bridge, North Carolina, March 20, 1865.
Cuckwold's Creek Bridge, South Carolina, February 8, 1865.
Culpepper, Virginia, September 14, 1863.
Culpepper, Virginia, October 12, 13, 1863.
Culp's Farm, Georgia, June 22, 1864.
Culp's House, Georgia, July 1, 1864.
Cumberland Shoals, Tennessee, January 13, 1863.
Cummings Ferry, Kentucky, July 9, 1863.
Cumberland Gap, Tennessee, September 9, 1863.
Curtiss Wells, Alabama, June 24, 1864.
Cross Roads, Virginia, November 26, 1863.
Cypress River, Tennessee, October 7, 1864.
Cynthiana, Tennessee, June 12, 1864.
Cypress Swamp, Georgia, December 7, 1864.
Dabney's Mills, Virginia, February 6 and 7, 1865.
Dallas, Georgia, May 24, 1864.
Dallas, Georgia, May 27, 1864.
Danbridge, Tennessee, December 24, 1863.
Danbridge, Tennessee, January 17, 1864.
Danbridge, Tennessee, December 25, 1863.
Danbridge, Tennessee, May 19, 1864.
Danburg, North Carolina, April 9, 1864.
Danville, Kentucky, October 17, 1862.
Danville, Kentucky, February 24, 1863.
Davis Cross Roads, Tennessee, September 11, 1863.
Dechard, Tennessee, July 4, 1863.
Decatur, Alabama, July 20, 1864.
Decatur, Alabama, October 28, 29, 30, 1864.
Decatur, Alabama, October 24, 1865.

Decatur, Alabama, November 28, 1865.
Decatur, Georgia, July 18 and 19, 1864.
Decatur, Georgia, July 20 and 21, 1864.
Deep Bottom, Virginia, July 27 and 28, 1864.
Devaux, South Carolina, December 9, 1864.
Double Bridge, Georgia, April 18, 1865.
Duck Pond Mills, Virginia, April 4, 1865.
Duck River, Tennessee, November 24, 1864.
Duck River, Tennessee, March 11, 1863.
Dug Gap, Georgia, May 13 and 14, 1864.
Durrant's Mills, Georgia, July 20 and 21, 1864.
Dutch Bottom, Tennessee, June 28, 1864.
Eagleville, Tennessee, January 20, 1863.
East Point, Georgia, August 3, 1864.
Eatonton, Georgia, August 1, 1864.
Elk River Ford, Tennessee, July 2, 1863.
Elk Water, West Virginia, September 11 and 12, 1861.
Ellistown, Mississippi, December 3, 1863.
Ely's Ford, Virginia, August 29, 1862.
Estillville, Virginia, ———, 1862.
Ettowa River, Georgia, May 24, 1864.
Ettowa River, Georgia, May 26, 27, 28, 1864.
Fair Oaks, Georgia, August 19, 1864.
Fair Garden, Tennessee, January 24, 1864.
Fair Oaks, Virginia, May 31, 1862.
Falling Waters, Maryland, July 14, 1863.
Farmington, Mississippi, May 9, 1862.
Farmington, Mississippi, May 5, 1862.
Farmer's Bridge, Georgia, May 15, 1864.
Farmville, Virginia, April 7, 1865.
Fayetteville, North Carolina, March 13, 1865.
Fitzhugh Crossing, April 29, 1863.
Five Forks, Virginia, March 30 and 31, and April 1, 1865.
Flat Rock, Georgia, July 27, 1864.

Flat Rock, Georgia, July 28, 1864.
Flat Creek Bridge, Tennessee, August 24, 1864.
Flemingsburg, Kentucky, February 18, 1865.
Florence, Alabama, October 6, 1864.
Florence, Alabama, October 10, 1864.
Ford, near Statesville, North Carolina, April 11, 1865.
Fort Esperanza, Texas, November 29, 1863.
Fort Saunders, Tennessee, November 29, 1863.
Fort Steadman, Virginia, March 25, 1865.
Fort Morgan, Alabama, August 23, 1864.
Fort Blakely, Alabama, April —, 1865.
Fort Hugar, Alabama, April —, 1865.
Fort Tracy, Alabama, April —, 1865.
Fort Pulaski, Georgia, April 14, 1862.
Fort Mahon, Virginia, April 2, 1865.
Fort Riley, Tennessee, September 1, 1862.
Fort McAllister, Georgia, December 13, 1864.
Fort Anderson, North Carolina, February 18, 1865.
Fort McGilvery, Virginia, April 1, 1865.
Franklin, Tennessee, December 12, 1862.
Franklin, Tennessee, September 27, 1864.
Franklin, Tennessee, November 30, 1864.
Franklin, Missouri, October 1, 1864.
Fredericksburg, Virginia, December 11, 12, 13, and 14, 1862.
Front Royal, Virginia, August 16, 1864.
Gainsville, Tennessee, Gebruary 19, 1863.
Gaines Mill, Virginia, June 27, 1862.
Gainesville, Virginia, August 29, 1862.
Gallatin, Tennessee, November 8, 1862.
Gallatin, Tennessee, April 13, 1862.
Gallatin, Tennessee, December 5, 1862.
Georgetown, Kentucky, June 13, 1864.
Gettysburg, Pennsylvania, July 2, 3, and 4, 1863.
Glasgow, Kentucky, December —, 1862.

Glendale, Virginia, June 30, 1862.
Golgotha, Georgia, June 15, 1864.
Goldsboro, North Carolina, March 22, 1865.
Grand Gulf, Mississippi, April 28, 1863.
Grand Gulf, Mississippi, May 27, 1862.
Graysville, Georgia, November 26, 1863.
Greenwich, Virginia, May 30, 1863.
Grenada, Mississippi, August 14, 1863.
Greenville, Tennessee, May 30, 1864.
Greenville, Tennessee, August 4, 1864.
Greenville, Tennessee, August 23, 1864.
Greenville, Tennessee, September 4, 1864.
Green Briar, West Virginia, October 3, 1861.
Gregory's Landing, September 4, 1864.
Griswoldville, Georgia, November 20, 1864.
Grovetown, Virginia, August 29, 1862.
Gunter's Landing, Alabama, May 15, 1862.
Hagerstown, Maryland, July 6, 1863.
Hagerstown, Maryland, July 10, 1863.
Hanover, Virginia, June 30, 1863.
Hanover, Virginia, May 27, 1864.
Hanover Court House, Virginia, May 27, 1862.
Harrisonburg Virginia, April 22, 1862.
Harrodsburg, Kentucky, October 10, 1862.
Harpeth River, Tennessee, January 12, 1863.
Harrison's Landing, Virginia, July 2, 1862.
Hatchie, Mississippi, October 6, 1862.
Hatcher's Run, Virginia, October 27 and 28, 1864.
Hatcher's Run, Virginia, February 5, 1865.
Hatcher's Run, Virginia, March 25, 1865.
Hatcher's Run Virginia, March 29, 1865.
Hawes' Shop, Virginia, May 28, 1864.
Haymarket, Virginia, June —, 1863.
Hazel Green, Kentucky, May 10, 1864.

Hazel Green, Kentucky, November 9, 1864.
Hazel Green, Kentucky, January 28, 1865.
Henryville, Tennessee, November 23, 1864.
Henry Court House, Virginia, April 8, 1865.
Hendersonville, North Carolina, April 21, 1865.
Hickory Creek, Tennessee, July 4, 1863.
Hickman's Bridge, Kentucky, March 27, 1863.
High Point, North Carolina, April 10, 1865.
High Bridge, Virginia, April 6, 1865.
Hillsboro, Tennessee, March 12, 1863.
Hill Creek, Tennessee, October 3, 1863.
Hillsville, Virginia, April 1, 1864.
Holly Springs, Mississippi, November 7, 1862.
Hollow Tree Gap, Tennessee, December 4, 1862.
Honey Hill, South Carolina, November 30, 1864.
Horse Shoe Bend, Kentucky, May 10, 1863.
House Mountain, Tennessee, January —, 1864.
Hoover's Gap, Tennessee, June 25, 1863.
Hudsonville, Mississippi, November 14, 1862.
Huff's Ferry, Tennessee, November 12, 1863.
Hunterstown, Pennsylvania, July 2, 1863.
Independence, Missouri, October 22, 1864.
Irish Bottom, Tennessee, October 25, 1864.
Island No. 10, Missouri, March 14 to April 7, 1862.
Iuka, Mississippi, September 19, 1862.
Jack's Shop, Virginia, September 26, 1863.
Jack's Creek, Mississippi, December 24, 1863.
Jackson, Mississippi, May 14, 1863.
Jackson, Mississippi, July 11 to 18, 1863.
James City, Virginia, October 12, 1863.
James Island, South Carolina, June 16, 1862.
Jamestown, Kentucky, June 2, 1863.
Jefferson Bridge, Tennessee, December 27, 1862.
Jenkin's Ferry, Arkansas, April 29, 30, 1864.
Jericho Mills, Virginia, May 24, 1864.

Johnsonville, Tennessee, March 25, 1864.
Johnson's Station, Tennessee, October 1, 1864.
Jonesville, Virginia, —— —, 1862.
Jonesboro, Georgia, August 19, 1864.
Jonesboro, Georgia, August 31, 1864.
Jonesboro, Georgia, September 3 and 4, 1864.
Jonesboro, Tennessee, March 25, 1864.
Jonesboro, Tennessee, April 5, 1864.
Jonesboro, Tennessee, September 30, 1864.
Jonesboro, Virginia, December 23, 1864.
Kelly's Ford, Maryland, September 13, 1863.
Kelly's Ford, Maryland, June 9, 1863.
Kelly's Ford, Maryland, November 7, 1863.
Kenesaw Mountain, Georgia, June 23 to 29, 1864.
Kenesaw Mountain, Georgia, July 1, 1864.
Kingston, Georgia, May 18, 1864.
Kingston, Tennessee, September 1, 1863.
Kinsboro Cross Roads, Tennessee, January 16, 1864.
Kingsport, Tennessee, June 18, 1864.
Kingsport, Tennessee, December 12, 1864.
Kingston, Tennessee, November 26, 1863.
Kirsville, Missouri, August 6, 1862.
Knoxville, Tennessee, November 18, 1863.
Knoxville, Tennessee, November 24, 1863.
Knoxville, Tennessee, July 24, 1864.
Knoxville, Tennessee, Siege of, September 17 to December 5, 1863
Lancaster, Kentucky, October 12, 1862.
Lancaster, Kentucky, July 30, 1863.
Lattimer's Mills, Georgia, June 20, 1864.
Laurel Mountain, Virginia, September 29, 1864.
Laurel Hill, Virginia, May 8, 1864.
Lavergne, Tennessee, January 1, 1863.
Lavergne, Tennessee, December 26, 1862.
Lawrenceburg, Tennessee, November 4, 1863.

Lawrenceburg, Tennessee, November 21, 1864.
Lawrenceburg, Kentucky, July 9, 1863.
Lay's Ferry, Georgia, May 14, 1864.
Lebanon, Tennessee, November 9, 1862.
Lebanon Mills, Georgia, July 14, 1864.
Lebanon, Kentucky, July 5, 1863.
Leetown, Virginia, August 25, 1864.
Leesburg, Tennessee, September 29, 1863.
Lenoir Station, Tennessee, November 12, 1863.
Lenoir Station, Tennessee, November 15, 1863.
Lexington, Missouri, September 12 to 20, 1861.
Lexington, Kentucky, June 10, 1864.
Lexington, South Carolina, February 15, 1865.
Liberty, Tennessee, February 20, 1863.
Liberty, Tennessee, April 3, 1863.
Little Laramie, Dacotah Territory, August 6, 1865.
Little Rock, Arkansas, Siege of, August and September, 1863.
Little Missouri River, Arkansas, April 3 and 4, 1864.
Locust Grove, Virginia, November 27, 1863.
Lookout Mountain, Tennessee, September 10, 1863.
Lookout Mountain, Tennessee, November —, 1863.
Lookout Valley, Tennessee, September 7, 1863.
Lost Mountain, Georgia, May 27, 1864.
Lost Mountain, Georgia, June 9 to 18, 1864.
Lost Mountain, Georgia, July 17, 1864.
Lost Mountain, Georgia, October 5, 1864.
Louden, Tennessee, September 29, 1863.
Louden, Tennessee, November 14, 1863.
Louden, Tennessee, September 2, 1863.
Louisville, Georgia, November 26, 1864.
Lovejoy's Station, Georgia, August 20, 1864.
Lovejoy's Station, Georgia, September 1, 1864.
Lovejoy's Station, Georgia, November 16, 1864.
Lumkins Mills, Mississippi, November 28, 1862.

Luray, Virginia, September 24, 1864.
McAffee's Cross Roads, Georgia, June 11, 1864.
McAffee's Church, Tennessee, September 19, 1863.
McCormack's Farm, Kentucky, September 23, 1864.
McCormack's Farm, Kentucky, November 10, 1864.
McCormack's Farm, Kentucky, December 29, 1864.
McDonough's, Georgia, August 20, 1864.
McGarvick's Ford, Tennessee, April —, 1863.
McMinnville, Tennessee, April 21, 1863.
McMinnville, Tennessee, October 4, 1863.
Macon, Georgia, April 20, 1865.
Macon, Georgia, July 30, 1864.
Macon, Georgia, November 21, 1864.
Magnolia Swamp, Virginia, June 1, 1864.
Malvern Hill, Virginia, July 1, 1862.
Manchester Pike, Tennessee, January 5, 1863.
Marion Tennessee, December 18, 1864.
Marietta, Georgia, July 1, 1864.
Marietta, Georgia, July 3, 1864.
Meadow Bridge, Virginia, May 12, 1864.
Mechanicsville, Virginia, June 26, 1862.
Mechanicsville, Mississippi, June 4, 1863.
Memphis, Missouri, July 18, 1862.
Middletown, Virginia, March 25, 1862.
Middletown, Tennessee, June 24, 1863.
Middletown, Tennessee, May 22, 1863.
Middleburg, Tennessee, December 24, 1862.
Middleburg, Virginia, June 21, 1863.
Madison Court House, Virginia, December 24, 1864.
Madisonville, Tennessee, October 30, 1864.
Mill Springs, Kentucky, January 19, 1862.
Millford, Virginia, May 27, 1864.
Milton, Tennessee, February 18, 1863.
Milledgeville, Georgia, November 24, 1864.
Mill Creek, Tennessee, December 25, 1862.

Mine Run, Virginia, November 26 to 29, 1863.
Mission Ridge, Tennessee, November 25, 1863.
Mobile, Alabama, Siege of, March 20 to April 12, 1865.
Monterey, Maryland, July 4, 1863.
Monterey, Mississippi, May 5, 1862.
Moore's Ridge, Georgia, July 12, 1864.
Moor's Mill, Maryland, July 28, 1862.
Morton's Ford, Virginia, November 26, 1863.
Morristown, Tennessee, December 10, 1863.
Morristown, Tennessee, March 19, 1864.
Morristown, Tennessee, June 2, 1864.
Morristown, Tennessee, August 3, 1864.
Morristown, Tennessee, November 20, 1864.
Morristown, Tennessee, December 2, 1864.
Morrisville, North Carolina, April 13, 1865.
Morristown, Kentucky, November 13, 1864.
Morristown, Virginia, December 25, 1864.
Morganton, North Carolina, April 16 and 17, 1865.
Morganton, North Carolina, April 18, 1865.
Morrisville, Virginia, December 30 and 31, 1862.
Mossey Creek, Tennessee, December 29, 1863.
Moses Creek, Georgia, October 3, 1864.
Mossey Creek, Tennessee, January 10, 1864.
Mossey Creek, Tennessee, December 26, 1863.
Mossey Creek, Tennessee, August 18, 1864.
Moseburg, Tennessee, June 23, 1864.
Moss House, Georgia, June 22, 1864.
Mount Crawford, Virginia, October 2, 1864.
Mount Pleasant, Tennessee, November 24, 1864.
Mount Sterling, Kentucky, June 9, 1864.
Mount Sterling, Kentucky, November 16, 1864.
Mount Sterling, Kentucky, January 19, 1865.
Mount Airey, Virginia, March 31, 1864.
Mount Airey, Virginia, December 17, 1864.
Mulberry Creek, Georgia, August 3, 1864.

Mumfordsville, Kentucky, September 14, 1862.
Mumfordsville, Kentucky, December 27, 1862.
Murfreesboro, Tennessee, July 13, 1861.
Murfreesboro, Tennessee, November 30 to December 20, 1864.
Metamora, Tennessee, October 5, 1862.
Nashville Pike, Tennessee, December 30, 1862.
Nashville, Tennessee, August 30, 1864.
Nashville, Tennessee, December 14 to 22, 1864.
Nashville & Chattanooga R. R., Tennessee, October 5, 1863.
New Madrid, Missouri, March 13, 1862.
New Hope Church, Georgia, May 25, 1864.
New Hope Church, Georgia, May 27, 1864.
New Hope Church, Georgia, June 1, 1864.
New Hope Church, Georgia, October 7, 1864.
Newton, Virginia, November 12, 1864.
New Market, Tennessee, December 25, 1863.
New Market, Tennessee, June 21, 1864.
Newport, Tennessee, July 8, 1864.
Newport, Tennessee, October 18, 1864.
Newton, North Carolina, April 17, 1865.
New Store, Virginia, April 8, 1864.
New Bridge, Virginia, May 24, 1862.
Nickajack Creek, Georgia, July 1, 1864.
Nickajack Creek, Georgia, July 5, 1864.
Noel's Farm, Virginia, May 26, 1864.
Nolansville, Pennsylvania, December 16, 1864.
Noonday Creek, Georgia, June 19, 1864.
Noonday Creek, Georgia, June 23, 1864.
North Vernon, Indiana, July 13, 1863.
North Anna, Virginia, May 23, 1864.
North Anna, Virginia, May 25, 1864.
Nottawa, Court House, Virginia, December 8, 1864.
Ny River, Virginia, May 9, and 10, 1864.
Ny River, Virginia, May 21, 1864.

Occoquan, Virginia, February —, 1863.
Ogechee, Georgia, December 5, 1864.
Opequan, Virginia, September 19, 1864.
Orange, Court House, Virginia, June 16, 1862.
Orangeburg, South Carolina, February 14, 15, 1865.
Orizaba, Mississippi, November 30, 1863.
Otterville, Missouri, October 10, 1864.
Overall Creek, Tennessee, December 7, 1864.
Owl Creek, Mississippi, May 17, 1862.
Ox Ford, Virginia, May 23, 1864.
Panola, Mississippi, July 20, 1863.
Paperville, Tennessee, December 13, 1864.
Paris, Kentucky, July 29, 1863.
Peach Tree Creek, Georgia, July 20, 1864.
Peach Tree Creek, Georgia, July 22, 1864.
Peach Orchard, Virginia, July 29, 1862.
Pea Ridge, Missouri, March 6 and 7, 1862.
Pea Vine Creek, Tennessee, September 17, 1863.
Peeble's Farm, Virginia, Septemer 30, 1864.
Peeble's Farm, Virginia, March 26, 1865.
Pegram Farm, Virginia, October 2, 1864.
Pelham, Tennessee, July 2, 1863.
Perryville, Kentucky, October 8, 1862.
Petersburg, Virginia, June 18, 1864.
Petersburg, Virginia, Siege of, June 17, 1864, to April 3, 1865.
Petersburg, Virginia, capture of, April 3, 1865.
Petersburg and Norfolk R. R., July 30, 1864.
Perryville, Kentucky, October 8, 1862.
Philadelphia, Tennessee, October 23, 1863.
Phillips Cross Roads, North Carolina, March 4, 1865.
Pickinsville, South Carolina, May 1, 1865.
Pierceville, Indiana, July 14, 1863.
Pigeon River, Tennessee, January 27, 1864.
Pine Hill, Mississippi, May 2, 1862.

Pine Mountain, Georgia, June 3 to 7, 1864.
Pine Creek, Tennessee, November 26, 1864.
Pittsburg Landing, Tennessee, April 6 and 7, 1862.
Po River, Virginia, May 10 and 11, 1864.
Pocotaligo, South Carolina, April —, 1862.
Point Pleasant, Missouri, March 9, 1862.
Point Burnside, Kentucky, August 30, 1864.
Pohick Church, Virginia, January 9, 1862.
Ponchatoola, Louisiana, May 16, 1863.
Ponchatoola, Louisiana, March 24, 25, 26, 1863.
Pond Springs, Alabama, June 28, 1864.
Port Republic, Virginia, July 26, 27, 28, 1864.
Port Gibson, Mississippi, May 1, 1863.
Port Jackson, Louisiana, April 25, 1862.
Port Hudson, Louisiana, siege of, May 23 to July 5, 1863.
Port Royal, South Carolina, Nov. 7, 1861.
Port Royal Ferry, South Carolina, January 1, 1862.
Port Royal, Virginia, April 23, 1863.
Poplar Spring Church, Virginia, September 30, 1864.
Pound Gap, Kentucky, May 17, 1864.
Powder Spring Gap, Tennessee, April 28, 1864.
Prairie Dehan, Arkansas, April 12, 13, 14, 1864.
Princeton Yard, Tennessee, January 6, 1865.
Princeton, Arkansas, December 8, 1863.
Prosperity Church, Tennessee, April 2, 1863.
Pulaski, Tennessee, December 25, 1864.
Purdy, Mississippi, Dec. 22, 1863.
Quaker Road, Virginia, March 31, 1865.
Raccoon Ford, Virginia, September 16, 1863.
Raccoon Ford, Tennessee, October 30, 1864.
Raleigh & Smithfield R. R., North Carolina, April 11, 1865.
Raleigh, North Carolina, April 12, 1865.
Rappahanock Station, Virginia, November 7, 1863.
Raymond, Mississippi, May 12, 1863.
Ream's Station, Tennessee, December 14, 1863.

Ream's Station, Tennessee, August 25, 1864.
Red Clay, Georgia, May —, 1864.
Red Oak Turnout, Georgia, August 27, 1864.
Reed's Bridge, Georgia, September 18, 1863.
Reinzie, Mississippi, August —, 1862.
Resaca, Georgia, May 9, 1864.
Resaca, Georgia, May 12, 1864.
Resaca, Georgia, May 13, 1864.
Resaca, Georgia, May 14, 1864.
Resaca, Georgia, May 15, 1864.
Rheatown, Tennessee, October 11, 1863.
Rheatown, Tennessee, March 24, 1864.
Richmond, Virginia, March 1, 1864.
Richland Creek, Tennessee, December 24, 1864.
Rich Mountain, West Virginia, July 11, 1861.
Richmond, Kentucky, —— —, 1862.
Ridges or Sailor's Creek, Virginia, April 6, 1865.
Ringold, Tennessee, November 27, 1863.
Ripley, Mississippi, November 29, 1863.
Robinson's Tavern, Virginia, November 29, 1863.
Rocastle River, Kentucky, October —, 1862.
Rock Island, Tennessee, August 2, 1863.
Rocky Face, Georgia, May 8, 1864.
Rocky Face, Georgia, May 9, 10, 1864.
Rogersville, Tennessee, June 17, 1864.
Rogersville, Tennessee, August 27, 1864.
Rome, Georgia, October 12, 1864.
Rome Cross Roads, Georgia, May 16, 1864.
Rossville, Georgia, September 22, 1863.
Rosswell, Georgia, July 4, 1864.
Rosswell, Georgia, Sept. 26, 1864.
Rough and Ready, Georgia, August 30, 1864.
Rough Station, Georgia, July 3 and 4, 1864.
Rover, Tennessee, June 23, 1863.
Rover, Tennessee, January 31, 1863.

Rover, Tennessee, February 13, 1863.
Rural Hill, Tennessee, November 15, 1862.
Rural Hill, Tennessee, December 20, 1862.
Russellville, Tennessee, December 12, 1863.
Russellville, Tennessee, December 2, 1864.
Rutherford Creek, Tennessee, May 10, 1863.
Rutledge, Tennessee, December 10, 1863.
Rutledge, Tennessee, December 15, 1863.
Sailor's Creek, Virginia, April 6, 1864.
Salvica, Kentucky, July 7, 1863.
Salvica, Kentucky, July 10, 1863.
Salineville, Ohio, July 26, 1863.
Salkehatchie, South Carolina, February 6, 1865.
Saltville, Virginia, November 20, 1864.
Saltville, Virginia, October 2, 1864.
Saltville, Virginia, December 20, 1864.
Saltville, Virginia, December 21, 1864,
Salem, Virginia, April 3, 1864.
Saluda Creek, South Carolina, February 16, 1865.
Sampterville, South Carolina, April 8, 1865.
Sandy Mountain, Virginia, October 3 and 4, 1864.
Sandtown Roads, Georgia, August 14, 1864.
Savannah, Georgia, December 11 to 21, 1864.
Savannah, Georgia, near, December 9, 1864.
Savage Station, Virginia, June 29, 1862.
Selma, Alabama, April 2, 1865.
Sevierville, Tennessee, January 27, 1864.
Sevierville, Tennessee, July 5, 1864.
Sevierville, Tennessee, September 18, 1864.
Seven Miles Ford, Virginia, December 19, 1864.
Sewell's Point, Virginia, March 5, 1862.
Sheperdstown, Virginia, August 25, 1864.
Shelbyville, Tennessee, June 27, 1863.
Sheperdstown Ford, Virginia, September 19, 1862.
Sheperdstown Ford, Virginia, September 20, 1862.

Shelbyville Pike, Tennessee, December 15, 16, 1864.
Shiloh, Tennessee, April 7, 1862.
Shoal Creek, Tennessee, November 5, 1864.
Siege of Atlanta, Georgia, July 22 to August 25, 1864.
Singleton's Plantation, South Carolina, April 19, 1865.
Smithtown, Maryland, July 6, 1863.
Smithfield, Virginia, August 29, 1864.
Smith Cross Roads, Tennessee, October 1, 1863.
Smith Cross Roads, Tennessee, August 21, 1863.
Smithfield Roads, North Carolina, March 18, 1865.
Snicker's Gap, Virginia, July 19, 1863.
Snicker's Gap, Virginia, November 4, 1862.
Snicker's Gap, Virginia, November 14, 1862.
Snow Hill, Tennessee, April 4, 1863.
Solemn Grove, North Carolina, March 10, 1865.
South Side R. R., Virginia, April 2, 1865.
South Edisto, South Carolina, February 9, 1865.
South Mountain, Maryland, September 14, 1862.
Sparta, Tennessee, December —, 1863.
Spangler's Mills, Mississippi, July 26, 1862.
Spanish Fort, Alabama, April —, 1865.
Sparta, Tennessee, August 9, 1863.
Sperry's Mills, Tennessee, August 17, 1863.
Spottsylvania, Virginia, May 10, 11, 12, 1864.
Spottsylvania, Virginia, May 18, 1864.
Spring Hill, Tennessee, February 29, 1863.
Spring Hill, Tennessee, November 29, 1864.
Spring Hill, South Carolina, April 15, 1865.
Stamford, Kentucky, October 14, 1862.
Statesville, Tennessee, April 22, 1863.
Stamford, Kentucky, July 31, 1863.
Statesville, North Carolina, Aprill 10, 1864.
Statesville, North Carolina, April 14, 1865.
Statesville, North Carolina, April 13, 1865.
State Creek, Kentucky, November 14, 1864.

Stevensburg, Virginia, November 19, 1863.
Steubenbille, Ohio, July 26, 1863.
Stevenson, Alabama, August 31, 1862.
Stewart's Creek, Tennessee, December 29, 1862.
Stilesboro, Georgia, October 11, 1864.
Stone River, Tennessee, December 29, 30, 31, 1862.
Stone Mountain, Georgia, July 18, 1864.
Stone Mountain, Georgia, September 13, 1864.
Stone River, Tennessee, January 1, 2, 3, 1863.
Strasburg, Virginia, March 27, 1862.
Strawberry Plains, Tennessee, January 22, 1864.
Strawberry Plains, Tennessee, August 14 to 17, 1864.
Strawberry Plains, Tennessee, August 24, 1864.
Strawberry Plains, Tennessee, November 23, 24, 1864.
Summit, Virginia, September 4, 1864.
Suffolk, Virginia, Siege of, April 22 to May 14, 1863.
Sugar Creek, Tennessee, December 26, 1864.
Summerville, Georgia, March 25, 1865.
Sun Shine Church, Georgia, July 31, 1864.
Swananoa Gap, North Carolina, April 19, 1865.
Sweet Water, Georgia, October 2, 1864.
Sweet Water, Tennessee, October 26, 1863.
Sweet Water, Tennessee, September 10, 1864.
Sweet Water, Georgia, July 3, 1864.
Swift Creek, South Carolina, April 17, 1865.
Salisbury, North Carolina, April 12, 1865.
Talladaga, Alabama, April 23, 1865.
Tebb's Bend, Kentucky, July 4, 1863.
The Crater, Virginia, July 30, 1864.
The Cedars, Virginia, May 2, 1863.
Thoroughfare Gap, Virginia, May 21, 1863.
Thompson's Station, Tennessee, March 5, 1863.
Thompson's Station, Tennessee, May 9, 1863.
Thorn Hill, Tennessee, September 10, 1864.

Thomson's Hill, Mississippi, May 1, 1863.
Thurley's Ford, Tennessee, December 15, 1863.
Tickfaw River, Louisiana, April 12, 1863.
Todd's Tavern, Virginia, May 8, 1864.
Tolopotomy, Virginia, May 30 to June 1, 1863.
Tolopotomy, Virginia, May 30, 1864.
Tazewell, Tennessee, —— —, 1862.
Tazewell, Tennessee, January 21, 1864.
Town Creek, Alabama, April —, 1863.
Town Creek, North Carolina, February 20, 1865.
Tiptonville, Missouri, March —, 1862.
Travillian, Virginia, June 11 and 12, 1864.
Trenton Gap, Georgia, March 22, 1865.
Triune, Tennessee, June 4, 1863.
Trion, Alabama, April 2, 1865.
Triplet Bridge, Kentucky, June 15, 1863.
Triplet Bridge, Kentucky, June 19, 1864.
Triplet Bridge, Kentucky, June 24, 1864.
Tullahoma, Tennessee, July 5, 1863.
Tullahoma, Tennessee, June 24, 1863.
Tullifinny, South Carolina, December 7, 1864.
Tunnell Hill, Georgia, January 28, 1864.
Tunica, Bayou, Louisiana, November 8, 1863.
Tunnell Hill, Georgia, May 7, 8, 1864.
Turkey Ridge, Alabama, October 26, 1864.
Turner's Ferry, Georgia, August 29, 1864.
Turkey Bend, Virginia, June 30, 1862.
Tuscaloosa, Alabama, April 1, 1865.
Unionville, Tennessee, March 4, 1863.
United States Ford, Virginia, January 1, 1863.
Utoy Creek, Georgia, August 4, 1864.
Utoy Creek, Georgia, August 6, 1864.
Versailles, Tennessee, June 10, 1863.
Vicksburg, Mississippi, May 20, 1862.

Vicksburg, Mississippi, siege of, May 19 to July 4, 1863.
Villa Ricca, Georgia, May 26, 1864.
Wadesboro, North Carolina, March 4, 1865.
Walker's Ford, Tennessee, December 2, 1863.
Wantahatchie, Tennessee, September 28 to October 28, 1863.
Wapping Heights, Virginia, July 21, 1863.
Wapping Heights, Virginia, July 23, 1863.
Wartrace, Tennessee, April 29, 1863.
Wartrace, Tennessee, June 3, 1863.
Ward's Farm, North Carolina, April 28, 1865.
Watanga, Tennessee, —— —, 1862.
Watanga, Tennessee, March 25, 1864.
Watanga Bridge, Tennessee, October 1 and 2, 1864.
Waynesboro, Georgia, November 28, 1864.
Waynesboro, Georgia, December 4, 1864.
Weams' Springs, Tennessee, July 27, 1863.
Weldon R. R., Virginia, June 22, 1864.
Weldon R. R., Virginia, August 19, 20, 21, 1864.
Western Virginia, October 5, 1864.
West Point, Virginia, May 7, 1862.
Westmoreland, Virginia, May 23, 1863.
White's Ford, Virginia, September 21, 1863.
White Pond, South Carolina, February 9, 1865.
White Horn, Tennessee, March 31, 1864.
Whitesboro, Alabama, June —, 1862.
White Oak Swamp, Virginia, June 30, 1862.
White Oak Swamp, Virginia, August 16, 1864.
White Oak Road, Virginia, March 29, 1865.
Williamsport, Maryland, July 6, 1863.
Williamsport, Maryland, July 12, 1863.
Wilderness, Virginia, May 5, 6, 7, 1864.
Williamsport, Maryland, July 10, 1863.
Willow Springs, Dacota Territory, August 12, 1865.

Wilson's Creek Road, Tennessee, December 11, 1862.
Wilson's Creek Road, Tennessee, December 21, 1862.
William's Ford, Tennessee, June 25, 1864.
Williamsburg, Virginia, May 5, 1862.
Wilmington Island, Georgia, April 16, 1862.
Wilmington, North Carolina, February 21, 1865.
Winchester, Virginia, May 23, 1862.
Winchester, Virginia, May 24, 1862.
Winchester, Virginia, August 11, 1864.
Winchester, Virginia, September 19, 1864.
Winchester, Kentucky, July 25, 1863.
Windsor, Virginia, May 22, 1863.
Winsted Church, Tennessee, December 13, 1864.
Wise's Forks, North Carolina, March 8, 9, 10, 1865.
Woodstock, Virginia, October 9, 1864.
Woodbury, Tennessee, January 22, 1863.
Wyatt's Ford, Mississippi, October 13, 1863.
Wytheville, Virginia, December 16, 1864.
Yadkin River, North Carolina, March 28, 1864.
Yellow Tavern, Virginia, May 10, 11, 1864.
Yorktown, Virginia, Siege of, April 4 to May 4, 1862.
Zollicoffer, Tennessee, —— —, 1862.
Zollicoffer, Tennessee, September 25, 1862.

FELL UNDER THE FLAG IN DEFENSE OF THE UNION, 1861-1865.

	OFFICERS.			MEN.			TOTALS.		
	Killed in action.	Died of wounds received in action.	Died of disease.	Killed in action.	Died of wounds received in action.	Died of disease.	Total officers.	Total men.	Total officers and men.
General officers, and on the staff, and in the regular service of the United States	1	3	3	----	----	----	7	----	7
In volunteer organizations of other States	2	3	2	----	----	----	7	----	7
1st Regiment Engineers and Mechanics	----	1	----	6	7	342	1	355	356
1st Regiment Light Artillery	4	1	3	33	10	367	8	410	418
1st Regiment Cavalry	10	5	5	92	46	246	20	384	404
2d " "	2	----	2	45	23	266	4	334	338
3d " "	1	2	4	24	8	375	7	407	414
4th " "	1	2	1	31	13	327	4	371	375
5th " "	4	1	3	94	23	233	8	350	358
6th " "	7	----	----	95	18	266	7	379	386
7th " "	2	2	1	47	24	246	5	317	322
8th " "	1	----	2	23	7	288	3	318	321
9th " "	2	----	2	23	3	151	4	177	181
10th " "	2	----	0	18	11	240	2	269	271
11th " "	4	----	----	18	6	114	4	138	142
1st " Infantry, 3 mo's	----	3	----	3	----	3	3	6	9
1st " " 3 years	12	3	1	103	32	92	16	227	243
2d " "	5	6	4	95	99	112	15	306	321
3d " "	4	----	2	96	47	75	6	218	224
3d " " re-organized	----	----	1	----	1	156	1	157	158
4th Regiment Infantry	8	4	1	115	50	95	13	260	273
4th " " re-organized	----	----	----	1	6	141	----	148	148
5th Regiment Infantry	10	6	3	141	75	163	19	379	398
6th " "	2	----	6	43	21	470	8	534	542
7th " "	6	5	3	123	47	154	14	324	338
8th " "	9	3	2	130	64	195	14	389	403
9th " "	2	----	4	11	7	268	6	286	292
10th " "	4	3	2	55	26	209	9	290	299

FELL UNDER THE FLAG IN DEFENSE OF THE UNION, 1861-1865.

	OFFICERS.			MEN.			TOTALS.		
	Killed in action.	Died of wounds received in action.	Died of disease.	Killed in action.	Died of wounds received in action.	Died of disease.	Total officers.	Total men.	Total officers and men.
11th Regiment Infantry	4	1	2	45	36	198	7	279	286
11th " " re-organized	----	----	----	----	----	81	----	81	81
12th Regiment Infantry	----	1	3	28	23	377	4	428	432
13th " "	3	1	2	40	30	314	6	384	390
14th " "	----	1	3	32	16	195	4	243	247
15th " "	2	1	4	48	18	264	7	330	337
16th " " and 2 Co's Sharp Shooters attached	10	2	----	155	48	128	12	331	343
17th Regiment Infantry	3	4	----	89	35	152	7	276	283
18th " "	----	----	----	11	2	297	----	310	310
19th " "	4	3	----	50	38	142	7	230	237
20th " "	10	3	3	64	37	173	16	274	290
21st " "	1	2	3	40	31	291	6	362	368
22d " "	1	2	3	52	27	289	6	368	374
23d " "	3	1	3	38	17	225	7	280	287
24th " "	12	1	2	118	38	142	15	298	313
25th " "	1	----	2	21	13	129	3	163	166
26th " "	1	2	3	61	37	155	6	253	259
27th " " and 2 Independent Co's attached	6	2	4	122	84	199	12	405	417
28th Regiment Infantry	1	1	----	4	----	122	2	126	128
29th " "	1	1	----	1	4	64	2	69	71
30th " "	----	----	1	----	----	17	1	17	18
1st Regiment Sharp Shooters	4	2	----	65	42	150	6	257	263
1st " Colored Infantry	2	----	1	4	5	128	3	137	140
Merrill Horse	0	----	----	2	6	67	----	75	75
1st Regiment U. S. Sharp Shooters	3	----	----	27	6	37	3	70	73
2d Regiment U. S. Sharp Shooters	----	1	----	9	3	18	1	30	31
Co. D, 66th Illinois Infantry	----	----	----	11	2	16	----	29	29
Co. A, 23d " "	----	----	----	2	6	10	----	18	18

FELL UNDER THE FLAG IN DEFENSE OF THE UNION, 1861-1865.

	OFFICERS.			MEN.			TOTALS.		
	Killed in action.	Died of wounds received in action.	Died of disease.	Killed in action.	Died of wounds received in action.	Died of disease.	Total officers.	Total men.	Total officers and men.
Co. B, 37th Illinois Infantry	----	----	----	2	1	2	----	5	5
Co. H, 42d " "	----	----	----	13	15	28	----	56	56
Co. B, 44th " "	----	----	----	9	5	29	----	43	43
Co. C. 70th New York "	----	----	----	15	3	7	----	25	25
In other companies serving in regiments of other States and in the regular army, so far as reported	----	----	----	----	----	----	----	14	*14
Taken from Roll of Honor U. S. Quartermaster Departme't as belonging to Michigan regments, but not found on regimental records	----	----	----	----	----	----	----	498	*498

RECAPITULATION.

Officers killed	177		
Officers died of wounds	85		
Officers died of disease	96		
		358	
Men killed	2,643		
Men died of wounds	1,302		
Men died of Disease	10,040		
	14*		
	498*		
		14,497	
			14,855

" Columbia e'er will know you
  From out her glittering towers,
And kisses of love will throw you,
  And send you wreaths of flowers,
And e'en in realms of glory,
  Shall shine your starry claims;
Angels have heard your story,
  And God knows all your names."

www.ingramcontent.com/pod-product-compliance
Lightning Source LLC
LaVergne TN
LVHW021422110826
845150LV00007B/2042